Living the Namaste Principle

A Unifying Paradigm Shifting Fear to Love

DOUG BILL

BALBOA
PRESS
A DIVISION OF HAY HOUSE

Balboa Press books may be ordered through booksellers or by contacting:

Balboa Press
A Division of Hay House
1663 Liberty Drive
Bloomington, IN 47403
www.balboapress.com
1 (877) 407-4847

Because of the dynamic nature of the Internet, any web addresses or links contained in this book may have changed since publication and may no longer be valid. The views expressed in this work are solely those of the author and do not necessarily reflect the views of the publisher, and the publisher hereby disclaims any responsibility for them.

The author of this book does not dispense medical advice or prescribe the use of any technique as a form of treatment for physical, emotional, or medical problems without the advice of a physician, either directly or indirectly. The intent of the author is only to offer information of a general nature to help you in your quest for emotional and spiritual well-being. In the event you use any of the information in this book for yourself, which is your constitutional right, the author and the publisher assume no responsibility for your actions.

Any people depicted in stock imagery provided by Getty Images are models, and such images are being used for illustrative purposes only. Certain stock imagery © Getty Images.

Print information available on the last page.

ISBN: 978-1-9822-1223-0 (sc)
ISBN: 978-1-9822-1221-6 (hc)
ISBN: 978-1-9822-1222-3 (e)

Library of Congress Control Number: 2018911189

Balboa Press rev. date: 10/03/2018

I dedicate this book to my beloved grandson, Elliott, born November 8, 2016, in the hopes that he and his generation will be the harbingers of the Namaste Principle.

Contents

Foreword

We are on the cusp of a pervasive shift in how we live on Planet Earth. Perspectives that were limited to a small group of seekers a generation ago have, little by little, crept into the mainstream. Between 2012 and 2016 the number of yoga practitioners jumped 50%. Another survey in 2016 suggested that in the next year 80 million people would try yoga for the first time.

Meanwhile, 40% of Americans say that they meditate at least weekly – another 8% say a couple times a month and 4% say several times a year. That adds up to 52%! Such numbers of people would have been unthinkable several decades ago!

Trends like this seem to indicate a movement toward a different paradigm of consciousness – a shift away from the primacy of the ego and away from cultural goals such as consumerism and competitive struggles to amass a fortune. Yoga and meditation are designed to lift us into a serene state, one that reveals our commonalities, the unitary consciousness that is our underpinning. However, despite our deep resonance with the truth of such paths, we are faced with the daily necessity of operating in a world that is mostly founded on quite different assumptions.

In other words, the next step for us is to apply in our daily lives what we are absorbing from such spiritual practices. What we need is guidance in how to do that.

This little book is a primer in one very simple and elegant way to bring a profound, spiritual truth into a hectic world. That technique is based on the common word used to greet others in south Asia: "Namaste." Hidden within the word is a world of wisdom and revelation. For it means: "I pray to the divinity within you." Or, phrased differently: "The divine within me greets the divine within you." If we say this enough times, and do so in a heartfelt way, we begin to settle into the truth of "we are both one in the divine," that is, "we are two waves on the same ocean." An ocean is much more significant, much larger, and more powerful than any individual wave in it!

How do we move out of the mindset of being little (or even BIG) waves unaware of our underlying connection? Waves that fade and disappear into nothing? The Namaste Principle brings our awareness back to our oneness each time we encounter another person...much as we bring our minds back to the focus of our meditation (a sound, the heart, the breath)....and then, when it wanders, bring it back again... and again....

Each person we meet in life's many rooms becomes, not an adversary, not a competitor, but a reinforcement of our common divine identity. And our lives begin to morph into something new.

Doug Bill gifts us all with a reminder of this revolutionary principle, and generously shares with us his adventure in discovering and re-discovering it, uncovering bit by bit, the profundity of the truth that it reveals...And he invites you into your own adventure of embracing the Namaste Principle.

Swami Ravi Rudra Bharati
Dancing Shiva Retreat Center
Black Mountain, NC

Acknowledgements

The writing of this book has been a multi-faceted process involving considerable input from many people toward whom I am deeply grateful. My wife, Risë, whose support and encouragement prompted me to begin this project, has patiently helped me to keep the vision alive over a period of 10 years.

Foremost among those who have cultivated within me the impressions that have blossomed into the Namaste Principle are my parents, Les and Jane Bill. Under their guidance and presence, my three older sisters and I were provided with an extraordinary flow of opportunities to experience many cultures, places and concepts that enriched and challenged our absorbent minds in countless ways.

The appearance of Swami Rama in my life at a time when I most needed to become grounded was immeasurably life altering. His teachings and personal guidance for me were critical in establishing my life's path. Eventually, as life would have it, encountering his human frailty led me to delve into the essence of the Namaste Principle – forgiveness.

The guidance of Ken Wapnick, Ph.D., whose unassailable integrity and clarity as a teacher of *A Course in Miracles*, helped me to navigate the complexities of the Course and instill in me what the true meaning of forgiveness is. His teaching not only assisted me through an existential crisis but helped establish within me a strong, psycho-spiritual foundation.

The mechanics of writing this book was a collaborative effort.

As I was struggling to get my ideas organized, my friend Jae Merrill, suggested I do a podcast. Not having a clue what that was, I proceeded to meet with Jae every two weeks, with recorder in hand, while we discussed the Namaste Principle. He posted our talks on a now defunct website.

Then, another friend, Kelly McMasters, a journalism professor and author of *Welcome to Shirley*, agreed to begin organizing the podcast material into a chapter format. After some time passed, our lives went different ways and we stopped working together on the material. Then again, after some years of the book lying dormant, another friend, Jan De Pinto, a freelance writer/editor, interreligious minister and spiritual director, resurfaced in my life after a 30-year hiatus. She has been the person to help me bring the book into its final form – in her own words, "carrying it over the finish line."

Many others – teachers, friends, supervisors, colleagues and especially my clients have been instrumental in guiding me to see the light within all of us. In the last chapter of this book, I've highlighted the main books and thought systems which have most inspired me in the formation of *Living the Namaste Principle*.

Introduction

The menacing, mobster-like man's eyes burned into the back of my head as J. spit out his question for a second time.

"What are you going to do about it?"

Everything froze for a moment. The words may as well have been venom. J. loomed in front of me like a giant, his lips pulled away from his teeth in a sinister smile. He was goading me, testing me, and I knew it. He had just loudly challenged me in the rec room, the most public arena possible at the locked down unit. I needed to decide how to react, and I needed to decide fast.

I could feel the other residents looking at me. PB., a notoriously tough man with a violent personality, watched quietly. I realized that the way I chose to react to J. right now could potentially set the tone for the rest of my time on the job.

We must have made an amusing picture: J., a hulking, muscled, dark-skinned man, standing aggressively over me – a minister's son, fair-skinned, slight of build with a soft voice that could barely rise to a yell even when I wanted it to. I had just started working at the facility as a psychiatric security aide while finishing up my graduate coursework in Eastern Studies and Comparative Psychology. I had a wife and new baby daughter at home and although I'd worked some nursing jobs before, this was my first experience with this type of population.

The other aides on the floor had warned me about our patients— some of whom were suicidal and many of whom were sociopathic.

The staff told me they were manipulative, violent, untrustworthy, and that PB. was the worst. He had a presence which ruled the floor like the Italian mobster in the movie *The Godfather.* I looked around for another aide in case I needed help. I had not yet earned the trust of many of the psychiatric aides, who were all veterans and who presented a much more intimidating presence than I did. At 25 years old, I was one of the youngest staff members on the floor, and since I was just 5 feet 8 inches and barely 150 pounds, I was not first choice for back-up when needing to subdue an out of control 300-pound, psychotic, violent patient.

Most of the interactions I'd witnessed on the floor were the result of a dichotomous, "us-versus-them" relationship between the patients and the aides. Proving domination was the key operant and words quickly dissolved into physical violence. I didn't have that option—there was no way I would be able to physically dominate J.— but I also didn't want to. *Namaste,* I thought to myself, relying on my meditative and yogic practices to ground me. *The divinity in me recognizes the divinity in you.* Calmly and quietly, I told J. I wanted to get to know him better, and asked him a personal question about his life.

J. looked puzzled. Then the muscles in his neck, which had been strained and tight during our confrontation, relaxed. I continued, starting a conversation, treating him as I would any other human being I wanted to get to know. I didn't curse, or yell, or threaten – dehumanizing behaviors likely more familiar to him. Instead, I treated him with respect. PB. kept a close eye on us as the conversation in the room returned to normal, the rest of the patients sensing that the danger was averted, and they wouldn't be watching a fight between us anytime soon.

This is the moment the Namaste Principle was born in me. I wouldn't name the concept for years to come, but looking back, this is the first moment in my life that I can see the imprint and power of the principle coming to life. I realized later that it had been some time since J. had been regarded as a human worthy of respect, much less a divine being worth getting to know. I went from viewing him as something *apart* to literally *a part* of me. With just this simple change of world view I was able to diffuse this potentially violent situation.

Lesson 1: A Part instead of Apart

> *A miracle is a service. It is the maximal service you can render to another. It is a way of loving your neighbor as yourself. You recognize your own and your neighbor's worth simultaneously.* – A Course in Miracles: The Advent of a Great Awakening [1]

But I had gained more than a friend in J. that day. I gained the trust of PB. Shortly after, PB. approached me requesting to learn more about the yoga and meditation principles he knew I studied. He was suicidal and depressed—he'd recently tried to end his life, but he was unsuccessful. An alert staff member had intervened and was able to get him medical assistance just in time. Upon coming to me, the more we talked, the more I realized this big, tough guy was like a ghost – defeated, empty of spirit.

PB. was one of the best arguments for suicide I'd ever met. As a patient confined to the facility with no hope for release, he had very few reasons to live and many reasons to want to die. He'd left a family on the other side of the walls with whom he had very little contact. He was an introspective man and the nature of his confinement was especially tough on him. We started discussing the principles of Raja Yoga—non-violence, honesty, surrender, and more—and how he might integrate these into the rough reality of his confined life.

Over the next nine years that I worked as an aide at the locked down unit, and then another four years as a vocational services worker, PB. went back and forth from one unit to another and we continued our discussions. He confided in me about his past and shared how he'd been on the streets since he was a teen, witnessing and participating in violence, drugs, alcohol, and sex. PB. was very receptive to the ideas and concepts I shared with him. He read books I lent him and made a sincere effort to practice the guiding principles therein. One book which had relevance for him was Bo Lozoff's *We're All Doing Time*.[2] Speaking directly to the prison population in his book, Lozoff has become an exceptional resource for anyone searching for a way to survive the oppressive stressors of any kind of confined life. PB. was able to more fully comprehend and practice yoga and meditation thanks to Lozoff's capacity to make the concepts of Raja Yoga relevant and easily transferable to addressing the challenges of a confined life. Over the years I watched PB. evolve while he continued to struggle with suicidal considerations. He blossomed a bit each time he returned to a much-needed reprieve from a severe mental health episode. It was impressive to see his way of taking the more vulnerable patients under his wing, using heartfelt compassion instead of force to divert others from disparaging behavior and unrelenting victimization of those who were defenseless. Of course, his bulging, tattooed muscles and reputation as a formidable presence helped as well.

By the time I retired from public service, PB. learned to recognize his own divinity – yoga means union of the little, individual, ego-based, limited self with the larger, universal, cosmic Self. He learned to recognize the divinity within those people around him: soon, not just residents, but security guards came to him for long talks and advice. Through PB. some of the psychiatric aides also came to trust and believe in me and my way of doing things.

Several years later during an evaluation, one of the supervisors pointed out that my presence diminished the tension on the unit because of my unique connection with the patients. There were fewer incidents of violence during my shifts because I helped to create an atmosphere of calm. I had begun to break down that poisonous "us-versus-them" mindset and instead promoted oneness and community.

I often refer to PB. as being one of my best students. After my work at the unit, I continued to hone what would soon become the Namaste Principle. As a therapist, I found myself counseling many children, individuals and couples in their attempts to overcome obstacles in their own lives, both emotional and situational. My clients were not happy—often they had lost the ability to communicate with those closest to them, making them feel utterly and terribly alone and unsupported. And usually, they had lost confidence and belief that they would ever feel happy and connected again. The people who sat in my office all seemed to have one thing in common—like PB., they'd lost their ability to recognize the divine being within themselves.

My quest to awaken, access and embody the awareness of the divinity within was both personal and professional. At the time, I was struggling with my purpose, drifting from one therapy job to the next, feeling frustrated. I found myself worried: How could I answer the needs of my clients when I couldn't find the answers for myself? I reflected on this idea, pondering how I could effectively bring my clients—and myself—to a new understanding of the self/Self and its relationship to the world. I knew that if I could help someone like PB., I should be able to help anyone. Then I realized that *was* my purpose: I needed to create a set of principles that would help people orient from a new paradigm, one that would work to cultivate a caring, compassionate community.

The Namaste Principle

Chances are that you've picked up this book for the same reasons I found myself moving from job to job, relationship to relationship and the same reason my clients find their way into therapy. Perhaps, something is missing in your life. Perhaps, you want to feel strong and loved again, loved by those around you and loved by yourself, as well. This begins with understanding that we are all connected and the first step to loving others is to love oneself. We are each a mirror, reflecting what is both good and harmful in ourselves onto others. If we are in pain, we cause pain. If we love ourselves, we love others. That connection is what has been missing.

The Namaste Principle is simple—we are reflections of one another, eternally connected. Derived from ancient Sanskrit, *Namaste* basically means, "I recognize, I honor the divine light within you." The idea is that one divine being is recognizing another, working off the principle that everyone—every single person on the planet—is a divine being. So, not just yoga teachers, or the Dalai Lama, or the person volunteering at the food pantry is a divine being -- *everyone* is a divine being. That includes the boss you don't get along with; the sour cashier at the grocery store who always packs your groceries haphazardly and squeezes your bread; your in-laws; and the big, aggressive personalities in the world like that of PB. and J. Everyone is connected and *everyone*—whether they know it or not—has the spark of the Divine within them.

Lesson 2: Recognize the divinity in everyone.

There is a game we should play,
And it goes like this:
We hold hands and look into each other's eyes
And scan each other's face.
Then I say,
"Now tell me a difference you see between us."
- from *I Heard God Laughing: Renderings of Hafiz* [3]

Imagine a world where every person respects the people around them, where no one views the world through a hierarchy of worth. By recognizing and respecting the spark of the Divine in yourself, you are much more apt to recognize and respect the dignity of others. So much of our worth in our world today is tied to material possessions—who has the most and who can get more are the people oftentimes in the limelight of society, especially Western society. But the true riches are within us, often invisible behind the façade of the latest title or award, fashion, gadget or car. Only when we realize this, can we cultivate a community grounded in love – looking beyond the many facades we wear to that timeless place where we are one.

Of course, it is unrealistic to expect an entire country or state or even family to be able to put the Namaste Principle into practice. Yet, in my experience, cultivating this principle produces outcomes which are quite contagious. I promise that if you commit yourself to the Namaste Principle, others will not only notice and want to be near you who embody such a presence, but eventually, will want to emulate you. And before you know it, you will be cultivating a community of people that is warmer, richer, and more connected to one another than before.

Inside this book

In this book, you will find tools to move toward a loving and non-judgmental acceptance of others as you clarify the essence of your own self/Self. Imagine your life as a house with each room signifying a particular important relationship. We will move from room to room, offering concrete and practical advice for ways to employ the Namaste Principle in your life.

The book is designed so that each room builds upon the other, but you can also feel free to enter and exit the rooms in whatever order you please. If you feel you are having the most trouble connecting with your partner, head directly to the bedroom. If you feel stuck at work and feel your success is stymied by a lack of respect in your workplace, head to the office.

You will also find sub-headings such as "Story," "Challenge," "Goal," and "Practical Application," which describe real life situations; common, inherent challenges in those situations; possible intentions or goals one might have to transform those challenges into opportunities for greater satisfaction and happiness in life; and suggestions or practices for fulfilling such intentions and goals. We all could learn how to communicate more effectively from a place of respecting ourselves and others more deeply. Stop and ask yourself right in this moment: *how might I and others benefit from non-violent communication and mutual respect and self-care?*

So, welcome to the Namaste Principle. I recognize and honor the divine light in you. Join me on an exploration into Light. Enter this house for all peoples!

Meditation Room

Story

I sat on the airplane, alone, staring out into the endless ocean below. A deep fear penetrated my body. I couldn't see land anymore and I realized, for the first time since planning my trip to Europe that I was completely untethered, with no safety net. I began to realize that I had set myself up for what might be a miserable failure. Although I had a vague sense of where I wanted to go, I had no real plan. I didn't even know where I was going to stay that first night.

As I was approaching Paris on my first overseas flight, I found myself becoming rather anxious about how I would begin my European journey. Most of the travelling I had done growing up was with my family. My mother always carefully planned our itinerary. As my parents, three older sisters and I piled into our station wagon heading off for a month of camping in state and national parks, I simply enjoyed the ride!

This pattern changed once I dropped out of college and began to carve out a more independent lifestyle. Between jobs, I would have a destination, but the itinerary was rather fluid – hitchhiking doesn't lend itself well to exact timing or even specific routes. It did, however, allow me to stretch my savings while meeting some fascinating people who were kind enough to help me get to where I was going. It also afforded me the opportunity to provide companionship to these strangers and even share some of the driving along the way.

In those days, though, I was on familiar ground – travelling cross country to visit family and friends presented no real threat. Some may consider hitchhiking rather risky but for me, the experience was always pleasant. It prepared me for the adventure in which I was now travelling to another continent, to Paris, where my only contact was a high school friend who was completing a university, year-abroad program in Bologna, Italy. Without a clue as to how I would get from the airport to Paris or where I would stay that night and without any fluency in French or any other language except English, I felt panic start to overtake me.

We've all had this feeling at one time or another. Fear is the most debilitating emotion on the planet. Fear keeps us from seeking out new experiences, new places, new people, and even time alone with ourselves. Being alone is perhaps the scariest thing of all for a human. Alone, there are no distractions, no busywork, no conversation. Alone, you are forced to face your own limitations, your weaknesses, and your powerlessness. This can be terrifying for modern humans, yet it can also be incredibly liberating.

Only once you come to know your weaknesses and limitations can you truly learn your own strengths. And only when you are able to be alone—truly alone with your deeper self—can you then come together with the rest of the world. This is the first foundation of the Namaste Principle: *Before we can learn to love one another, we must learn to love ourselves.* In order to do this, we must accept that we are not in control of everything, and that is okay.

We have to trust that our deeper self knows what we need and is following a very detailed map, even if it feels sometimes like we've lost our own GPS. Only then can we move from a fear-based to a love-based perspective.

Reflecting further on that moment, I recognize how, in a very real sense, I was about to graduate from one level of trust into a much more expansive level. Yes, I was sinking into a fairly fearful state: "Will I survive the abyss of the unknown that lies before me? How, with all my limitations and insecurities, will I get through this unscathed? Yet, was I really a separate entity, isolated and alone, without any means of support beyond what my frail humanity might pathetically muster?" These fearful doubts swirled around in my heart and mind, but the journey I had undertaken would soon teach me otherwise!

As the plane landed, I simply followed the flow of travelers as they made their way to a bus stop and signs to Paris. At this point, I noticed two guys my age with long hair who were smiling and seemed friendly. As I introduced myself to them, they reported that they had met on the plane, were from Canada, and had made plans to share a hotel room in Paris. When I asked if I might join them, they happily agreed. We proceeded over the next three days to enjoy the extraordinary sights of Paris such as the Louvre, Montmartre, and the Eiffel Tower, and then went our separate ways. Separate but not alone or isolated – this was becoming ever clearer to me.

My next stop was Bologna. Although I travelled by train, I chose not to use the three-month EurailPass I had purchased before leaving the States as I journeyed on. Z., my friend attending university abroad, showed me the sights of Bologna and nearby Parma and Reggio Emelia. When he discussed his plan to travel through Eastern Europe, where my EurailPass was not valid, I told him I would like to join him. Glad to have me as his travelling companion, he said we could start in one month when his semester would end. In the meantime, I decided to check out the Greek islands.

After hitchhiking to Brindisi and boarding the ferry to Corfu, I made friends with two more long-haired hippies who had been travelling Europe together and were on their way to India -- a trip that could be made for less than one-hundred fifty dollars at the time. I sent Z. a letter informing him that I would not be joining him in Eastern Europe after all, but that I was on my way to India!

The next four months elevated and expanded my perspective

in so many ways, that I find it difficult, if not impossible, to fully express how this occurred within the parameters of this book. Very simply, I experienced a process in which I entered a "flow state." My own decision-making faculties were historically confined to the more habitual, daily functions we all rely upon to live. Beyond that, I found myself in a river-like current that coursed through one fascinating adventure after another.

One of my college roommates was from India, and I thought perhaps I could contact his family when I got there. I didn't expect him to be there but thought it might be nice to have a friendly face somewhere in the unknown. Again, I just knew I wanted to go there. So I changed course and followed my new travel companions.

We made our way to Istanbul and found a 1960 Mercedes bus that was going as far as Katmandu. The bus, whose sides were emblazoned with the words "The Bus", took the scenic route— through Turkey, over to Iran, Afghanistan, and Pakistan and finally, for me, New Delhi. There were people from all over the world on the bus—Argentina, Australia, New Zealand, France, and Germany. We were moving from one adventure to another and became quite close, camping out on beaches off Turkey's southern coast at night or in the deserts of Afghanistan. The seats were removed from the bus, and during the day we all rode packed in like sardines, trading paperbacks and talking at length, watching the incredibly lush landscape go by.

Once I got to India I wrote a letter to my roommate's parents, saying I was a friend and was planning to travel through their town, Indore, on my way to Bombay and that I'd love to visit. They invited me to stay, but when I arrived they told me there had been a death in the family and invited me to travel to the Ganges River to help scatter the ashes. I followed them to the foothills of the Himalayas and was so moved by the sacred mantras and rituals. What's more, they invited me into this intimate process. I knew I wanted to learn more about their world. I wound up living with their family for a month. This month changed the course of my very existence.

India is where my education truly began and where my eyes were opened to the power of meditation. If I'd allowed fear to take over—if I'd never left the airport in Paris and turned around and came home on the next flight; if I'd stayed in the comfort of Western Europe instead of going to Greece; if I didn't hop on that crazy bus that bounced all the way through the Middle East over to India—I'd never have experienced what turned out to be some of the most profound moments of my life!

I was not in charge of where I was going. I began to trust in the divine presence and relinquish control. Something was directing me—just as something is directing everyone else on this planet. In choosing to put myself in such a tenuous situation, I allowed myself to just float and let that divine presence take over.

Living in India cultivated a loving state within me. I knew I'd only scratched the surface, but that's what I was left with—the way people responded to each other. In spite of their poverty they were rich, and their intent was so deep. They surrendered to the Infinite.

My roommate's mother meditated daily at her *puja* table, a kind of small desk for devotions and offerings. I wouldn't really learn how to meditate for another few years, but what I witnessed in India was meditation in action. The fruits of meditation played out around me and that's what I was responding to—people moved into each moment with mindfulness.

I was reminded of my meals at home with my family: when we said grace we would sit down and be focused on that kind of intentional thought and appreciation. We were suddenly mindful of our actions. This occurred over centuries in India and became a way of permanent being. It felt to me as if every moment was as mindful as our meals at home after saying grace at the table.

The connection between grace at my Christian minister father's table and my Hindu mother's *puja* table is an important one. This is the essence of the Namaste Principle: *we are all the same.* Our energy, our love, our beings are all connected. I had to travel to the other side of the world to gain this understanding. And to think—because of fear, I almost didn't make it! I could have stayed in Italy, or in America, for that matter. Yet, had I listened to that voice of fear instead of love, I never would have learned some of the most profound lessons of my life. Instead, I found my calling – all because I was able to approach my situation from a viewpoint of trust in a guiding force bigger than me instead of from the fear-based perspective of my small, ego self.

Challenge

If the Namaste Principle is about creating connectedness and promoting positive relationships, the most misunderstood relationship is the relationship with self. Often, we are so completely disconnected from ourselves that it is hard to imagine that we are also connected to something so much larger than ourselves.

Breaking out of that fear-based perspective can be incredibly difficult. Yet, the relationship with one's self is the most important to cultivate and this is where the change begins.

Goal

Let's start by defining our relationship with one's self. Initially, this may seem in opposition to a belief system like the Namaste Principle. Thinking about self may feel uncomfortable at first, or terribly self-centered. The idea that the relationship with one's self is the most important sounds self-absorbed, ego-centric, or exclusive of others.

In fact, it is quite the opposite. This is because the "self" we are talking about is the true Self—the Self that is all inclusive of the being-ness we share with one another. Understanding that one's Self is connected to everyone else's Self helps us to realize that other people are not the enemy, but in fact are a part of us—this helps dismantle and/or dissolve that fear-based perspective.

A healthy and respectful relationship with one's Self is the foundation of the Namaste Principle. An ingrained practice of mindfulness helps one achieve that experience of meditation in action in which I was enveloped while living in India – keeping the relationship to one's self connected and centered.

Practical Application

Find Your Meditation Room

I'm using the idea of the Meditation Room to reflect the solitude of the self, the self with whom you are left when no one else is around. This does not mean that you need an actual meditation room to apply the Namaste Principle to your life, or that you need to sit cross-legged for an hour or 20 minutes or even five minutes a day and meditate. Instead, think of the room as an opportunity to be alone with yourself, in whatever way works for you.

For an Indian mother, this meant sitting at her *puja* table in a quiet corner of her bedroom. For you, this might mean staring out the window with your cup of tea in the morning before everyone else wakes up, taking a few minutes to be by yourself in your car before you go into your office building, or going for a walk in nature after lunch. Wherever works best for you to quiet your mind and contemplate self is your meditation room.

Commit to Time with your Self

Life is complex. Often it feels like a wheel spinning around and around, all confusion and dizziness. Yet, in the Meditation Room, you become the hub of the wheel. The hub moves along with the wheel, but it is not spinning itself—the hub is not caught up in the craziness. When you are in the Meditation Room, you are living in the world, but not driven by the world.

In order to achieve the experience of meditation in action, mindfulness needs to become a way of being—not simply a way to calm down when stressed or on the weekends when you have extra time, although either of these reasons are a good starting place to a transformation of one's state of being. To feel this power within everyday life, one needs to practice mindfulness every day, multiple times. It's that simple. Making time for this is making time for yourself. Practicing mindfulness establishes one more firmly in being connected to one's self and to others.

Making the Ghee

As the son of a minister, spirituality has been a constant context in my life. Growing up, being involved in the church and community had much meaning for me. This is where I found connection – a sense of belonging to self and others – and this is what we human beings really long for and look for in various ways. What is required for establishing connection is being present to oneself and to others. Another word for this is mindfulness, and mindfulness is often referred to as a form of meditation. Later, as I moved into a period of practicing Raja yoga, I began meditating twice a day and teaching yoga and meditation.

A universal mantra used for meditation is "*So hum*", or "I am that." "That" signifies pure, eternal Beingness – divinity – in contrast to what we've been conditioned or trained to be—for example, a husband, a father, a therapist, a son. The practice of meditation, just like the Namaste Principle, is intended to bring us into a particular state of being. I liken this process to the refining of ego. Many people have the mistaken notion that ego is a bad thing, but this is not true at all. One just needs to put it in its proper place. Ego is not who we are, but a vehicle we are utilizing on life's journey.

In Indian cooking a lot of *ghee* – clarified butter – is used, and the effects of practicing the Namaste Principle on ego is much like the process of preparing *ghee*. One starts with the butter, composed of milk solids and fat. It's the milk solids in butter that cause the butter to spoil if left unrefrigerated and hence, the milk solids might be viewed as impurities. So, one places the butter into a pan on low heat and skims off the foam that rises to the surface as the milk solids separate from the milk fat as it transforms into a golden, clear liquid that settles at the bottom of the pot. This process is repeated while the pan is on low heat, so it doesn't burn—too low, and the milk solids will congeal and not separate from the fat; too hot, and the mixture will burn. The remains from the slow cooking process is only the butter fat – ghee, an amazing cooking oil which doesn't get rancid if left unrefrigerated. Ultimately, this is the essence of butter.

In the same way, the work done with the Namaste Principle in the Meditation Room will bring one closer to the essence of Self. This work will help clear away all the "foam," the veil over the true Self formed of the hardened identifications of self projected by the ego to protect itself. This is a process that takes time—we've been programmed to believe that we are the name we've been given, the sex our biological nature has, the personality, possessions, goals, and relationships that make up our life. This is not to suggest disposing of our ego, just making a clear distinction between Self and ego, moving into a way of being that draws upon that truth that we share—this divine essence.

What to Say

Catholics have the rosary, Muslims have *tasbih* beads, and the Hindus and Buddhists have the *Japa mala beads*. The main bead on the *Japa mala* is called the *Meru*, or guru bead, and they are to be held in a particular way in front of your heart and touched one at a time. Through the repetition of the movement and a chant, an evolution occurs, like clarifying the butter, moving one more directly to one's source, the essence of one's being. This is a guide to one's truth. The idea of *sutra*, which means string, like the string of beads, is that one is drawn toward truth following the thread of consciousness embodied in the chant (mantra). When meditating with these beads, I used the Gayatri Mantra, from an old Sanskrit verse:

Oh, Thou Supreme Lord Source of Existence, Intelligence and Happiness,

9

Creator of the Universe,
May we prove worthy of Thy choice and acceptance.
May we meet Thy Glorious Grace.
And may Thou vouchsafe an unerring guidance to our intellects,
And may we follow Thy lead unto righteousness.
Om Shanti, Shanti, Shanti.[4]

This is what I repeated when I first learned to meditate during my time at a yoga institute. I spent nine months living at the institute and meditating for hours a day. This is where I met my wife Risë, and later became a husband, then a father. After returning to the busy world outside the institute with its responsibilities, challenges, chaos and confusion, I continued to meditate and found that I was grounded more deeply in a detached witnessing yet engaged perspective towards life than I had ever been before.

This is where the concept of a meditation room without walls came from. Even if I didn't meditate for hours a day anymore, I still found a way to clear my mind and connect with my Self. This meditation practice became the foundation for the rest of my whole life. In a way, though I rarely sit for long meditative stretches anymore, I'm always, in a sense, in a state of mindfulness. By establishing the practice, moving out into the world is about always remembering that it's all God. Each person, each object, each event, each action holds the Divine within. The essence of all of us human beings is that we are all the same in our basic desires for happiness, belonging, purposefulness and survival, so that despite the appearance of separation and difference, the reality is that we are all one. Meditating helps us plug into that reality and serves as a daily reminder of our true Self.

This moving through the world and always remembering that it's all God is not easy, and I am still hard at work on this process. Again, returning to the analogy of ghee-making, if you take the perfectly purified ghee outside, leaving it uncovered and exposed to all the elements, it will attract all kinds of impurities and pollution from the environment – dust, bugs, and various particles. And just like the ghee, once you leave the meditation room and re-enter diverse arenas of the world, or turn on the TV, computer or radio, our hearts, minds, and bodies are impressed, if not outright assaulted, with how we are different from other people instead of how we are the same. It takes returning to that state of *at-one-ment* through meditation, day after day, continually refining that butter essence, to establish a mindfulness that reminds us that we really are all one.

Final Thoughts

The Meditation Room is the foundation of the Namaste Principle. The remaining rooms which we will explore in this book rest upon this solid base. Take time to implement this practice and you will find the next rooms considerably easier to build. We will refer to the Meditation Room from time to time as we continue through the rest of the house together.

Ideally, if you live the Namaste Principle, everything you think and say and do comes out of that essential truth, *So Hum*. This leads to a much happier state of mind and being. How we reach this state is up to us—a mountain has many routes to the top. Depending on your route, you may face different conditions than your neighbor. But the summit is where we are all trying to go—the truth, beyond words – a peace that surpasses all understanding. It doesn't matter how we get there or which route we take. I've described a very specific path here—my own—but this is certainly not the only one. I hope this helps you finds yours.

Awakening into Namaste

Decades ago in Katmandu, I journeyed to the East and had reached what I considered my highest point, being about 100 miles from the summit of Mt. Everest. Although it was certainly the furthest eastern point to which I would travel, I would soon discover my mind would enter even greater heights than the Himalayan peaks surrounding me.

The German commercial bus that would carry me back to New Delhi from Nepal had an interesting array of passengers, mostly European tourists. One passenger in particular, X., struck me as someone I needed to get to know. As I settled into the seat next to him, he described how he had just given farewells to his friends in the rock band Traffic, after travelling from Europe together on their tour bus. What most impressed me about X. was his calm, self-assured manner. He emanated a kind of fearlessness grounded in humility and he had a very precise way of expressing himself.

As our bus crossed into more level Indian terrain, X. offered me some "window pane" LSD. Although I had done trips on mescaline and had many experiences with different forms of marijuana, I had chosen to avoid LSD, thinking I was not ready for the intensity it might incite in the emotional and psychological dimensions of my being. However, knowing that "window pane" LSD, which looked like a tiny square of mica, was a rather pure form of the psychedelic drug, I accepted his offer. I thought to myself: now, after nearly four months of engaging in a flow of amazing adventures, it is the perfect time to experience the inward journey into which LSD might draw me. After placing the tab under my tongue as X. directed, I asked him how long the psychedelic trip would last – to which he replied, "For the rest of your life!" His response initially struck me as peculiar since the physical effect of mescaline usually lasted about eight hours. Now, several decades later, I understand the prophetic nature of his proclamation. In fact, I attribute the quality of my experience that day on LSD as the implantation of the seed of the Namaste Principle.

For what happened in that LSD trip was an expansion of my consciousness, an opening of the doors of perception and a deepening of the feeling of connection with those people around me when I stepped off the bus. We had stopped at a village for lunch and refueling the bus. The villagers quickly surrounded us with a consuming curiosity toward the Western strangers who had suddenly appeared in their rural town in their fascinating land. In broken English, one after another of these vibrant people asked me questions as to where I was from and to where I was going. The LSD was beginning to peak in my awareness, triggering its full intensity. The effect was a heightened clarity of all my senses and an energy coursing through my whole being that was nearly overwhelming in the enthusiasm I felt for life at that moment.

Years later, I would learn the origin of the word *enthusiasm* – that is, "en" means "in", "thusia" means "God".[5] On that day of the LSD trip, in that moment of meeting the villagers as the drug peaked, I *felt* the presence of divinity all around and within me: although a stranger in a strange land, I felt that no one was foreign, nothing was separate about the people around me who appeared no less than amazing to me – each of them revealing their unique holiness, their unique expression of incarnated divinity. Over the last three months of my travel in India and thereabouts, I had often heard the greeting *"Namaste"* presented by local inhabitants with upraised palms pressed together in front of their hearts. Again, I wouldn't really understand the original meaning and depth of that greeting – *The divinity within me prays to the divinity within you* – until a few years later during my studies at a yoga institute.

Returning to my Kathmandu journey, soon I was back on the bus, yet my mind was racing beyond the New Delhi destination we would soon reach. I was beginning to assemble the many pieces of my journey and a purposeful vision was burgeoning in my mind. Amidst the flow of "grokking in fullness"[6] moments which lingered after the LSD trip ended, along with the perfect backdrop of thoughts from Aldous Huxley's *Doors of Perception* and Alan Watts' *Joyous Cosmology*, my mind waxed grandiose as I envisioned a resolution of the world's problems with me as the one who knew how to make it all happen! Was this vision fallout from the LSD trip, just a common symptom of mental disarray or was it an outpouring of the transpersonal Self of which we are all a part, and which now dominated my vision? I claim the latter.

It would take decades to ground myself in understanding what this visioning was really about. I must say, however, that X.'s assertion that this trip would last for the rest of my life was so much more prescient than either of us could have imagined.

So, as my journey home to the States proceeded, I soon encountered one more situation which crystallized the meaning for me of what my travels to the East really portended. I was in the state of Punjab, not far from the India/Pakistan border in the city of Amritsar where the Golden Temple, sacred site of the Sikhs, was housed. Fascinated by this religious community of the Sikhs, I spent much of the day within the walls of this temple, where a moat-like pond lay, featuring a walkway to the temple. The Sikhs who greeted me were so friendly and welcoming and I enjoyed the privilege of participating in an amazing service there in the Golden Temple.

As I was departing from the temple, I met several, young men who had just crossed the border into India after traversing the same route I had taken from Europe three months prior. They described how they had fled their country after being captured and tortured by the military police that were part of a Fascist regime which had gained control of their homeland. As we talked further, I sensed their anger at what they had endured and their suspicion of any system they perceived as authoritarian. Espousing Communist concepts, they were all about "freeing the people." They, too, had just visited the Golden Temple and their perceptions of their experience there were quite different from mine. With a deep certainty that rang rather authoritatively (ironically), they shunned the kindness and welcoming nature of the Sikhs as a sham. The blessed food which the Sikhs had offered to us all – *prasad*, a sweet doughy concoction -- was a sign to them of how the Sikhs were attempting to seduce us all into accepting their spiritual path. As these angry, young men, in defense of their view, quoted Karl Marx, who referred to religion as "the opiate of the people", I redirected my attempt to dissuade them, realizing the futility of such a verbal disagreement. The contrast in our views of a commonly shared experience was a catalyst in further crystalizing what my journey East had taught me. My appreciation for this journey and my enhanced worldview only deepened.

The richness of the culture and the depth of genuine spirituality were inextricably linked to the hearts and minds of the vast majority of people with whom I had interacted along the way. There was a quality of Being that transcended religion – universally embracing. Of course, I encountered many individuals who lacked this quality. Sadly, there seems to be a growing trend of dissociating from the Eastern culture's spiritual roots as the attraction of Western civilization draws so many people away towards the evermore dazzling lure of things we can buy. The point is that there is another way. I had a glimpse of the essence of what this other way looks like on the journey east, yet years of training my mind and gaining a practical understanding of how to implement this way still awaited me.

The Namaste Principle is about one method of how to experience the genuine spirituality found at the heart of many wisdom and faith traditions. *Living The Namaste Principle* presents practical guidelines intended to be a springboard for the reader to consider how to best engage in the challenges each room of their life presents. As you will discover, there will be no real discussion of esoteric principles or concepts – only a common call in each chapter to embrace the unifying message of *"Namaste"* so as to reframe life challenges in a positive light. Rather than slipping into knee-jerk, fear-based reactivity, we will mindfully address the situation with kindness while remembering the divine essence within oneself and other. What emerges as a possibility from this approach is an allowance of love and forgiveness as our guides through perplexing life situations to achieve a win-win outcome for all persons involved.

The Family Room

Story

Like many homes in the past, the dinner table was the center of our family life. With two working parents and two busy kids, the dinner table was the one place where we were reliably together as a whole family, calm and centered enough to listen to one another's news or problems and look one another in the eye. This is where our family life was fed, physically and spiritually.

Since our work schedules required time out of the home and away from the children, we made sure to create certain patterns and lay a foundation of routine and trust. My wife and I both worked, and we were also focused on providing uncompromised love of family—both extended and nuclear. I didn't have a lot of time, but I had a lot of love, and I wanted a way to show my kids I loved them and to make them feel taken care of and to spend time with them.

As with most young children, nutrition was a constant concern. Especially when they were little, my wife and I had trouble encouraging our two children to eat healthy, balanced meals. Luckily, through experimentation, I hit upon a recipe that was both healthy and really enjoyable to the kids. One night, I made kid-friendly tofu burgers with a balance of vegetables and brown rice, and the kids gobbled them up. On the weekends, I'd make 60 or 70 burgers and freeze them (this was before the days of the ubiquitous frozen veggie burger section in the grocery store). These burgers were our quick, healthy, go-to meal when Risë and I were pressed for time or when the kids had to make a meal on their own as they got older.

Looking back, I realize now those tofu burgers offered more than simple food nourishment; they also nourished my children's confidence. During my weekend burger-making marathons, I put more than just healthy ingredients in those burgers. I put my love and care and concern into them. These simple burgers established a sense of trust and reliability—if they were ever hungry and at home alone, they could pull open the freezer and know that I had provided them with a balanced, healthy and delicious meal. These homemade burgers were one tangible way of taking care of my kids and showing them love. And my kids—on some level—knew that.

Challenge

When we were raising our children, pressures from the outside world threatening the stability of our family life were strong, but today they are even stronger. Parents with two or three jobs between them, overscheduled kids, fast-food, and television and cellphone screens all compete for our attention. In most families today, the tether that bonds us together gets lost. It is no wonder.

Holding a family unit together is hard work, even when the intention is there. Holding a family unit together when there is no intention to start with makes it an impossible task. Many of us today are simply running from one appointment to another, without attention to the thread of intention that connects each act and the teaching opportunities in the stuff of daily living. Kids need a base and a routine—something they can depend on. Nothing elaborate is needed, no fancy gadgets or trips. But something as simple as having dinner as a family every night, or at least most, nights is incredibly powerful.

Parenting today is also wrapped up in a lot of guilt, especially when both parents work. Many parents think they need to attend to their children's needs first and subsume their own personal needs. "My kids come first!" is a mantra one can hear over and over again. But if you always put your children first—whether it be their schedules or desires or emotional needs—you are in danger of losing yourself, losing your vitality and withering away. Without you, children cannot get any of their needs met—this is why we ask caregivers to place their own oxygen masks on their faces first in airplanes and then turn to the child next to them. If an adult is depleted, they have nothing left to give to the child. It is important to carve out time to attend to personal needs and holistic matters first, so that you can be there for your kids as your full self. Imagine yourself as a first responder at a fire—you must be certain of your own preparedness before entering the burning building and attempting a rescue.

In this day and age, many families are in financial crises, and so much work leaves less time for the children. So many parents, single and partnered, spend the majority of their day stressing out about bills, filling the gas tank, and paying the mortgage and credit cards down, that they lose sight of why they are sacrificing so much in the first place.

In my own experience, creating a routine that allowed the dinner table to be the center of our family life took a lot more effort than it might seem. Both Risë and I were committed to establishing a family-centered home, one that honored us as a unit, and we worked hard from the very beginning of our lives together to retain this focus.

But even with both adults in the house working toward this goal with intention, holding that dinner table time and space was often incredibly difficult. We decided early on that even though many of our clients preferred evening and weekend office hours, we would only open our practice during weekdays. We would have benefited financially, but we felt the cost to our family life would be too great.

Not every family is in the fortunate position to dictate their own working hours, of course, but the kitchen table is just an example— there are many other ways to focus on the family in an intentional, reliable, daily way that will strengthen and nourish the unit.

Goal

The most loving parenting perspective I have found is not to expect children to do or not do what YOU think they should or should not do. Reframing one's parenting role from benevolent dictator to something more like a guide can help remind oneself that one's foremost goal as a parent is to teach this fully-formed being how to move along in this world, and the next. Ideally, the role of the parent is one of support and mentorship, not forced shaping.

One thing to keep in mind is the idea that your children are not your children.[7] They are coming through you, but not to be dominated by you. They are their own people and look to you for guidance and mentoring. Of course, it is important to teach practical things, like reading, math, and good hygiene. Yet, parents also need to put an emphasis on spiritual values. Look for ways to model and teach love, kindness, compassion, honesty, and trust. If you are generous with your child as well as others, and if your child witnesses your generosity, she will be able to understand and recognize generosity and express it in her own life.

If this love-based (as opposed to fear-based) type of parenting feels exciting, but you're not sure where to start, take advice from Covey and "begin with the end in mind."[8] The best way to turn around old patterns is to begin with a sense of purpose and intention. Imagine your family sitting together at the dinner table, listening and interacting with one another in mutual respect: then, take the steps to make that happen. If schedules won't allow dinner, perhaps breakfast is the venue for your time of connecting and checking in with one another. Transform your thinking — transform your life! This is where it all starts.

Practical Application

Self-care First

For a chapter focused on family, it may seem strange for the first recommendation to appear to be self-centered in nature. Yet, self-care is not the same as being self-centered in a selfish way. The parent is the bedrock of the family, and if that bedrock isn't solid, the family falls apart. Self-care isn't selfish—it is necessary for the well-being of the individual and communal well-being, in this case, the whole family.

Now self-care doesn't mean putting one's self first. It simply means caring for the self spiritually, physically, and emotionally in the process of expending energy caring for others. Nourishing the self makes it possible to nourish others. Simple things like getting enough sleep, regular exercise, eating a balanced diet and some form of spiritual practice all help to build a strong base from which a healthy family tree can grow.

For parents with partners, it is important to be on the same page about priorities. For single parents, knowing your priorities is equally important. When parents bring their baggage – that is, habits, attitudes, rules of conduct learned from their own family milieu – they may find themselves in conflict with each other. Something as simple as the proper way to squeeze toothpaste from its tube can become a point of contention! It would reduce the potential for much unnecessary stress, if parents would agree to sit down together occasionally to consider what their shared goals are in child-rearing and parenting. For example, if they realize they both want their children to get through meal time happy and well-nourished, they may find it easier to dispense with or modify certain rules with which they each grew up. Should their child or children eat everything on his or her plate or should the child or children simply give each food a chance by taking a taste of each food on the plate? Reviewing and discussing learned rules from their own childhood which both parents bring to child-rearing and planning in advance on commonly agreed rules to which they will both adhere, will eliminate confusion on the part of the child(ren) and reduce the possibility of any youthful attempts to play one parent against the other.

In this way, parents truly work together as a team, as one force of the presence of love which brought them together as a couple in the first place, and which naturally seeks expression in their connection with their children. From the perspective of keeping one's eyes on the prize, so to speak, of parenting – although this may vary in expression from one family to another – it is helpful, if not necessary, to remember the long-term goal of parenting – essentially, to nurture children in a manner that engenders strength, confidence and independence as they prepare for and enter adulthood.

Grounded more and more in the Namaste Principle, parents will find that their presence reflects the empathy and respect with which they regard all life. The example they thus model for their children may serve to instill a similar appreciation of and regard for the shared divinity within us all in the hearts and minds of their children.

Single parents face unique challenges, yet the process of staying grounded in love based on the Namaste Principle, and emulating this as daily parenting situations arise, will support the single mother or father in staying on track with his or her goals to instill strength, confidence and independence in his or her children. When parents are separated and sharing/co-parenting their children, it's crucial that they transcend their differences to cultivate consistent, loving strategies to nurture their children.

Whether parents are living separately or under the same roof, or if only one parent is involved, it is useful and important to take time to stand back and look at how the job of parenting is playing out. Mindfulness Meditation, a form of self-care, embodies this process of standing back and looking and is an invaluable tool, not only in parenting, yet in life as well.

Deeply Engaged Time

With clear priorities and a strong regimen of self-care, time can be reserved for the kind of regular, deep engagement children crave. This doesn't have to mean spending hours in the kitchen cooking veggieburgers. Find your own way to spend consistent, focused time with your children.

Dinner time is a perfect opportunity to cultivate togetherness. Keep the television and cell phones off and use this time to really be present to one another. Talk about your day, what was good and what was bad, things to be grateful for as well as anxieties. There doesn't need to be a set agenda—the talking isn't the important part, but the listening is key. Give your kids your full attention and this will build trust and convey to them how important they are to you.

Reading before bed is another way to be close to your child. Reading to infants while holding them close, creates warmth and safety first and a favorable impression of books, which can lead to a lifelong love of reading. Even when it seems they might be too young to understand what you are reading to them, they are experiencing closeness, intimacy, and safety and associating this with your voice and gentle physical touch. This is the feeling you want to foster with your child throughout their young life: that you are a pillar of security, someone to be relied upon, whose love and affection is constant.

Seek First to Understand

Stephen Covey's fifth of the *7 Habits of Highly Effective People* offers parents another particularly valuable tool: "Seek first to understand and then to be understood."[9] This suggests a process of conveying a sincere interest in what another is feeling, thinking, experiencing. Rather than arbitrarily imposing our will upon our children, as parents we are wisely advised to listen deeply to them. As we gently inquire as to what's going on in the mind and heart of our child, he or she will sense the love prompting these questions and the dialogue that unfolds can reveal what often evolves into a deepening mutual respect and understanding. This especially arises as we "connect the dots" of the bigger picture which appears as our child responds to our inquiry.

We then might find our own perspectives changing, perhaps becoming less inclined to condemn "bad behavior." As we share our concerns and feelings about the matter at hand, we might also happily find a way of "synergizing" – Covey's sixth habit which entails a way of joining together that expresses how the whole is greater than the sum of its parts.[10] Thus, conflicts we initially encounter in a parenting situation can be resolved in a mutually respectful manner, without domination.

The Bedroom

Long-lasting and satisfying marriages and healthy relationships in general, are clearly an endangered species today. Much of the reason for this has more to do with the individuals involved rather than the couple they create by being in relationship.

When two people join, through marriage or a commitment ceremony or simply by mutual agreement, our culture often sees this as the crowning act of union. However, joining with another person is a process—you don't magically go through the ceremony of a wedding, say "I do", and then become joined as one. Rather than as an ending, we should think of this as just the beginning of a very long and sometimes joyful, sometimes painful process of merging together.

Ideally, as your personal development unfolds, your relationship changes and grows with you. Marriage is not a static act, but a continual work-in-progress. And even if a couple is perfectly in tune, the ups and downs of life can easily destabilize even the strongest bond. Work is required by both parties, but the work is beneficial.

Story

My wife Risë and I had an unusual opportunity to meet and grow into our relationship slowly. Tasked to work together on a project at the yoga institute, we engaged in deep and meaningful conversation over the course of months before our relationship became romantic. We had the luxury of walking for hours, talking about the universe, our beliefs, and our hopes and dreams. This was the foundation of what has become a marriage of 40 years.

Those 40 years have not always been easy. When thinking about the long-view of our relationship, I'm reminded of a trip we once took to Moosehead Lake, Maine. During this trip, a friend had given us specific directions to find a place known for moose, an animal we were excited to see. We took our kayak out on the lake and pulled the boat to shore where our friend suggested. We strayed away from our course when the moose weren't in that spot, and hiked around until we did see a small family of majestic moose, their breath steaming in the early morning. Our trip was a success and even magical. But now, it was time to find our way back.

Risë trusted me to get us back to the lodge. There had been talk of rain and wind coming, and we'd spent more time than we'd planned out in the forest, searching for the moose. We found the kayak and got back in as the skies darkened and the wind picked up. The lake was choppy, and I started tacking — taking the boat right into the waves —zigzagging back and forth, with the waves and against them. In the back of my mind, I knew if our kayak was broadsided by a wave we were likely to go under, and I'm sure this was in Risë's mind, too, but I tried to keep calm and Risë dug in as my partner on the boat. We were riding those waves together.

We both trusted that we would make it. Risë trusted in my skills to get us back home, but I couldn't have done it alone. She was paddling away, so I needed to trust in her strength. We also had to trust that this would be an adventure, not a disaster. And while it took us four-times as long to make it back, the skies didn't open up until we'd pulled our kayak out onto the sand and we were safe.

The act of navigating the lake together, our shared enjoyment and physical rush, was a kind of sacred renewal for our relationship, even after nearly four decades together. While much of our trip offered opportunity for serene reflection, there were moments that were flat out terrifying. We knew that at any moment we could get crushed against boulders or stranded, turned upside down and dumped out of the boat, but when we were able to skillfully navigate our way through the danger spots, our trust—in ourselves and in one another—grew.

Much like our relationship, we know the lake will mostly consist of deep, easy flowing waters. But even in the most peaceful moments, we also know that up ahead there may be storms we'll need to face. There is no such thing as a ride that is always peaceful and smooth – in marriage or kayaking! Before we get into that boat each time, we know we may be facing disaster. And in the midst of that disaster, we may be totally drawn into the drama of the rocks and rapids, forgetting that we've been here before and that it worked out well in the past.

In our marriage, each time we get into the boat of a new life challenge, we carry with us the uncertainty of what lies ahead – rocks, rapids, or unperturbed waters. And after riding together for nearly 40 years, we know that even if some horrible disaster is splitting us, we trust that we're going to make it back to the shore together.

Challenge

When two people stand next to one another and agree to join lives, the work of surrendering the ego is just beginning. Unfortunately, in our culture today, so much emphasis is placed on the fanfare of the wedding day that this is often seen as a finish line, not a starting place. But marriage is a process—not just a ceremony. The hard work actually begins after the wedding.

Marriages today face an inordinate amount of strain. Outside pressures and temptations mixed with internal fissures and faulty foundations account for marriage's terrible track record in our contemporary culture. Many of the most common problems faced by couples in committed relationships are the result of the kind of fear-based misunderstanding of the world that the Namaste Principle is built to heal. Here are some examples of issues that tend to tear couples apart:

- *Individual Ego*: Ego is a wild horse; it has much energy and power, but when not directed, ego can do an incredible amount of damage. The process of capturing a wild horse usually involves either love or fear. The idea of "breaking" a horse, forcing the animal to submit and be dominated by a hand it fears, is one way of understanding the undercurrents of many failed relationships. Jealousy, possessiveness, and control are a few of the ways we try to force our partners to remain in a relationship with us. But to what end? If we break the spirit of the person we love, what is left?

In the movie *The Horse Whisperer*, Robert Redford had a different take on how to tame a horse. Instead of using a whip, Redford came from a place of kindness and love. In this story, Redford built a relationship with a severely injured horse suffering from Post-Traumatic Stress Disorder. Other trainers had tried and failed to revive and control the horse, but through love the Horse Whisperer was able to bring that horse back to balance. That's what we need to do with ego—our own and our partner's: bring it to balance.

But how can one tame ego? *Surrender.* The answer is the same whether an ego is under-developed and you or your partner suffers from low self-esteem and lack of nurturance or if the problem is the opposite and an ego is over-developed, resulting in an egocentric response to the world and an overblown sense of self. Either way, there is a distortion at work.

Creating marriages based on various fears means that for many, there isn't a surrendering that is inherent to marriage. Instead, we set up walls right from the beginning with pre-nuptial agreements and a "what's mine is mine, what's yours is yours" attitude. This pre-nuptial mentality puts up a wall that then is always there, disrupting the ideal that is intended to be a joining together as one and surrendering to the love that unites us. All too often such marriages end up sadly as divorce statistics.

- *Infidelity*: As with many addictions, we perceive the problem of our own unhappiness to be externally produced. So the solution must be out there if the problem is out there. People think to themselves: *My spouse is the problem, so I will take another lover and resolve that problem.* Often, they feel justified and blame their spouse for not meeting their needs in the first place. But of course, infidelity isn't a solution: instead, it simply compounds the problem. In the case of infidelity, partners need to accept that the issues are not external, but internal. And when working through cases of infidelity, the focus should not be about blame and innocence, but rather on the faulty foundations that caused the rift in the first place.

- *Other addictions*: We will deal with other addictions that are not specific to marriage but that create difficulty in marriage in a later chapter called "The Rooms."

-*When surrendering is impossible: Divorce.* Certain spiritual traditions look upon divorce as a sin. The Namaste Principle does not. As a therapist, I've dealt with couples where the health of the marriage was so damaged it was impossible to repair. What I look for is a willingness to engage in the process, to ultimately surrender. If there isn't a shared willingness to do the hard ego work, divorce may be the only option for the people in that marriage to achieve a deeper sense of joy or satisfaction, perhaps through a partner better suited, but certainly through individual work and self-love. If a marriage is loveless, something needs to be changed. Therapy can help you rise above that state of "lovelessness", but a willingness to engage in this deep process of self-inquiry is required by both parties.

Goal

The Third Entity of Marriage: How the joining of two equals three.

In our contemporary culture, often marriage is represented as two entities becoming one. But a healthy marriage leaves room for both people as individuals while creating space for a new third entity, the partnership. Instead of diminishing or eliminating aspects of the individual for the sake of joining together, the most successful relationships allow the partners to cultivate each one's individuality and hence, these relationships grow and expand.

Risë and I came from very different worlds; Risë was raised in a Jewish family in an urban area with a deep emotional connection, a very loving, caring, passionate family. I came from the middle of the country with a Christian minister father and learning about Rise's family showed me for the first time how emotionally disconnected my family actually was. We did all of these things together—took month-long vacations together, talked of spirituality and politics, but there was no real, free flow expression of emotion in my family. It was very constrained — not negative, just restrictive.

Before Risë and I met, though, my own family evolved as my three older sisters and I moved into adulthood; as a foursome, we grew in our understanding of the conditioning that influenced our personal development. Whenever we were all together we would talk about our family's issues. As adult siblings, we became aware of the restrictive parenting we received as children and the effects this had upon us. Then, a few weeks after our marriage, Risë joined the conversation at a holiday gathering at my parents' home. Together, we looked at the dynamics of our familial relationships, often finding our flaws as amusing as they were disturbing. Risë's presence in our lives certainly brought another dimension, and for me at least, brought greater clarity to my sisters' and my understanding that what shaped us need not contain or limit us. As adults looking back at our childhood with a more critical eye, my sisters and I had begun the process of self-inquiry which forms the essence of psychotherapy. I accepted Risë's observations of my family dynamics; we were able to discuss these observations without condemnation on her part, and without defensiveness on my part. As a couple we share the liberating experience of discovery without the sharp edge of judgment.

Surrendering to another person and accepting and embracing a state of vulnerability takes courage. But we need to unlearn the fear-based thinking we've been taught and instead do our best not to perceive others as a threat, especially those we love. Through loving ourselves, and building loving relationships, we can learn to awaken the deeper sense of love that unites us all.

Each of us walks around this earth with a hard, protective shell around our hearts. You'll know you've gotten the Namaste Principle down when the shell cracks open – again and again. We all live inside this hard shell, and when we aren't ready it is very difficult to break that open. When we're ready, it almost just falls off on its own. With this shedding occurs a deep sense of trust and oneness that is so joyful. The trust in one another transcends the individuals – the third entity, the partnership, is bigger than both of us.

Practical Application

Learning about yourself through your partner.

When Risë and I entered into our relationship, the first years required frequent translation in dialogue. Raised in very different families, we grew up guided by different standards and expectations, and distinct ways of perceiving the world. The way one approaches things will be different, anything from squeezing the toothpaste to handling money. Yet, differences don't have to come between and divide you from your partner. When faced with a difference of opinion and approach, use it as an opportunity to explore your own opinions and approach with curiosity and wonder rather than resistance to the differences in another's viewpoints. Even after 40 years, Risë and I are still growing and learning, about one another and about ourselves. The work is ongoing.

The Mirror

Blame is a main component of failed or failing relationships. Often, I only see a problem in others because it is invisible and not acknowledged in me. *You're not giving me what I want, so maybe we should just hang this up*—this stance assumes the problem and solution are external. However, we need to recognize that the "issues" with our partners are often just a mirror reflecting back to us the rough or wounded edges of our being.

True listening can help overcome the tendency to hide. Most of us want to hear only what we want to hear, but, in truth, we need to learn to truly listen. When we're really hearing what another is saying, we become a mirror image of another's light or darkness, building walls of separation, or merging and dissolving in connection and oneness – friends, rather than enemies -- no longer coming from ego. Discussions are no longer attacks, but calls for love.

I have often used the following technique designed to promote the skill of deep listening between couples whose relationships are "on the rocks." In his book *Getting the Love You Want*, psychologist Harville Hendricks presents practical guidelines as part of what he calls Imago Therapy; one of these exercises is called "mirroring" in which the couple is asked to recount an incident to each other, one of which the other is unaware.[11] After the story is relayed, with the specific sequence of events and the resulting feelings expressed, the other will respond with: "This is what I heard you say…." Then, after the story is reflected back, the one who first told the story will say: "Well, you got most of the story, but you missed this part…and you didn't say how I felt when that happened…." (Both individuals have been cautioned before doing the exercise not to editorialize" what they heard the other person say, that is, not project their own judgmental impressions of what they just heard, but simply to state what they just heard.) Once the mirroring has been done to the satisfaction of the reporter, the roles are switched, and the second person tells their story which is reflected and corrected as needed until the second person is satisfied that they were heard accurately.

The couple is then asked to practice this way of communicating as a type of study assignment between therapy sessions. Over time, the couples with whom I have worked and who have practiced this technique, have made significant gains in improving the quality of their communication and the relationship itself.

The Workplace

We all know these two types of people in the office: the first are the ones you never want to get caught next to at the water cooler because they drone on about their overtime or broken desk chair, or rope you into gossiping about a co-worker, or simply rain on your parade. They hate their job and they aren't afraid to let you know it. They are like Eeyore from the classic Winnie-the-Pooh books, the people who feel like dark clouds that soak you if you get too close.

But chances are you can also recognize a different type in some offices: the upbeat optimists, the man who always asks others about their day, or the woman who is always smiling, as though she has a secret life outside of work that is so wonderful she can't contain her happiness. They seem to love their job, regardless of whether they are drinking coffee at a café or sitting in the corner office. These are the people you hope you get to sit next to at work luncheons, the ones who make you feel like they bring the sunshine inside with them, even if you are all tucked into your tiny cubicles all day.

You've probably felt like both in your past—I know I have, and sometimes I have felt like both types of these people on the same day. But I used to feel primarily like the first kind of person – that is, until I figured out that the key to being more like the second has nothing to do with the office or the job.

Story

In early 2010, my job as a child and family therapist at a mental health agency was wearing me down. My caseload was immense, and I was typically booked six weeks out. I spent most of my time dealing with bureaucracy, and primacy was placed on treatment plans and other paperwork since this was the way the budget for the agency was assessed. I found the system inefficient, dysfunctional, and completely frustrating. And I was miserable. I thought the system needed to change in order for me to be peaceful, and I felt helpless because I knew I couldn't affect any change in this behemoth. I was ready to quit.

As summer was nearing, an opportunity presented itself to work as a mobile therapist, going into the homes of kids and families who needed therapy assistance and working one-on-one with parents and their children. I spent that summer driving around, feeling useful and hopeful. The job was great, and my supervisor was fantastic.

As summer drew to a close, however, I realized I was spending an inordinate amount of time getting caught up on paperwork at home. Evenings and weekends were spent catching up on reports I wasn't able to complete because of the time I spent on the road during the day. I realized I couldn't afford to keep this job, even though I enjoyed it so much more than my other position. I had to make a choice: either stay with a job I enjoyed but couldn't afford, or return to a job that made me miserable and be prepared to simply tune out and trudge through the days of the week until the weekend came.

But neither of those options seemed livable to me. Instead, I made a conscious choice to return to the difficult job with a whole different outlook. I came to understand that I was the one who needed to change.

Rather than needing to change the system to make it more therapeutically oriented, I just had to do what I could in that little world of my own. I needed to accept that the system was broken.

Once I wasn't expecting sanity, competence, or an integrated therapeutic system, I was finally free to just focus on what I could do. I could not change the world, but I could change my perspective. After I made this change, I never felt as overwhelmed as I had in the previous years. Changing my dysfunctional environment was an impossible task—I was setting myself up to fail. And failing over and over again, on a daily basis, had worn my spirit down. Understanding that I had the power to change myself by making changes on a daily, incremental basis was empowering.

Changing my perspective also made me change the way I understood the system. As part of protocol, I was required to update every single one of my treatment plans every three months. For a long period, I found this requirement infuriating. These priorities seemed completely askew—the system was intended to provide quality treatment. But after I changed my perspective, I made a choice. There was a way of working within the system to make that happen. I decided to engage in the process and promote change in the treatment plan. I could see "these people" and "this system" as the problem. Or I could see that by making it an issue, *I had become the problem.*

So instead, I began to see this process as an opportunity. I saw the treatment plan as a small piece of the change. I started to view the process as a way to check in with my patients and check in with myself. Rather than view the quarterly reports as stifling or as a way to keep me under someone's thumb, I saw them as a way to genuinely interact with my clients and chart the progress we had made. This often became the most rewarding aspect of the treatment process. Being able to celebrate a success or make a new goal was exciting and helped to remind both the client and myself that we were actively engaged in a process of growth and change.

Much of what we discussed during the treatment plan update was meeting the goal of the need to consistently and lovingly impose natural, logical consequences to behavior. We looked at ways my patients could stop doing things that worked against their happiness.

I also applied this to my own life. When I got caught up in the craziness of the bureaucracy and the broken system, I stopped doing my work. Instead, I worked to move more deeply into what I could change. What I *could* control became my focus, which was much more satisfying. Instead of dealing with a dysfunctional system, I connected with my work.

By simply changing my perspective, one of the worst parts of my job turned into one of the most rewarding. By the time I left my job, I was no longer escaping it. I wasn't overwhelmed, and it wasn't the source of my unhappiness. I no longer perceived the need for all these changes. It was still the same place, but I was a different person. I was at peace. I knew I had done what I could within myself. I had created a state of inner peace. And I was ready to move on—instead of running away.

Challenge

In our modern world, the idea of job satisfaction has become an unrealistic dream. So many people today live for the weekends simply because they don't believe it is possible to find contentment, much less pleasure, in their daily work. A large part of this dissatisfaction is the result of feeling powerless—powerless over a demanding boss, or a cruel co-worker, or an unfair or inefficient system. Yet we all must work in order to live our lives. Often, instead of trying to find a solution, we give up. We surrender to the inevitability that work is a drag and something through which we must simply suffer.

Much of our default processing leads to judging others or our situations. Instead of taking responsibility for what we can, our natural tendency is to place blame externally, on those outside of ourselves—like that unrealistic boss or inefficient billing process. This also in effect transfers our personal power to those things or people. We are giving them the power to make us miserable. And giving away your personal power adds more misery on top of that original misery.

Goal

But what if instead of perfection, we began to see the perfect in the imperfect? What if, instead of focusing on what this job is taking from us, we focused on what more we could give to our own personal work experience? What if we asked ourselves the question: How am I able to find peace in this moment?

Practical Application

Self-Care

Our jobs may dictate when we must arrive or clock out, but it is our own responsibility to coordinate a daily routine to consciously allow for self-care elements. For example, most offices are sedentary places. If you have an hour for lunch, you can choose to walk for 30 of those minutes and eat for the other 30 minutes. Often, big corporations have their own work-out facilities or a reduced rate at a local gym. Taking care of your body and mind is just as important as getting to work on time.

Meditation

Since most of us work outside of our home, our work life feels separate from our home life. But the office—regardless of where it is physically located—is still a part of our *house*. And when one room in our house is neglected, it impacts the entire house. In every room, the practice of meditation is going to promote the capacity to see the divinity within others. This is because the process of meditation is leading us to see that divinity in ourselves.

Find a place or time that makes the most sense for you to meditate at work. This could mean in your car before you enter, or during a break, or simply in a private moment at your desk. Aim for once a day, and then move up from there. Find what works best to set your own equilibrium.

The Classroom

In order to learn, humans must feel safe enough to open their minds and hearts. But in our current society, the classroom has increasingly become filled with anger and aggression. The anxiety and fear that permeates our schools is hurting our children—physically, emotionally, and spiritually—and making true learning all but impossible.

Statistics and cover stories have forced us to act, and these days zero-tolerance policies and anti-bullying programs abound. We're throwing weight and money around to try and fix the problem, but what if we are simply making it worse? So far, the rapid influx of these programs has not worked to staunch the meteoric rise in violence and threats, both in the schoolyard and cyberspace.

This is because all of these programs have one thing in common: they bully the bully. We need to embrace the bully's victim, of course, but if we only do this we are ignoring half of the equation. Until we can come from a place of love, for both the bully and her victim, we'll simply stay stuck.

Story

Several years ago, a young woman named S. was assigned to me at the counseling center. She had inherited a mood disorder from her father, who had been hospitalized a couple times, but overall her parents were incredibly supportive. As a unit, the family already had a self-care structure in place, focusing on communication, healthy diet and exercise, and working together to face issues that came up within their household.

But one day, S. came to me with a problem she was having in school that she had so far been unable to resolve. There was another girl in her class who was bullying her relentlessly, making fun of her and bringing friends into the process. S. already physically stood out—she was very tall, easily the tallest girl in her class, and she was also large. This girl who was picking on S. had keyed in on her propensity to feel like an outsider because of her physical presence and was pushing it to the limits.

This hurt S., but her self-esteem was strong enough to sustain this kind of attack. Instead, S.'s main concern was her reaction. She did not want to allow this girl to antagonize her past her breaking point—her size made her stand out from her peers, but it also made her a very real physical threat. S. knew that if things got physical and she wasn't able to control her temper, she could really hurt this girl. S. had come to me in self-preservation, but amazingly, she was also seeking help in an attempt to protect her tormentor.

S. already had enough self-respect and esteem to stand up for herself, a tribute to the support system her parents had built at home. She was able to pair this ability with some key components including communication skills I taught her in our sessions and then apply them to her situation. I talked with her about Marshall Rosenberg's *Non-Violent Communication*[12] principles and suggested S. let the girl know what she was feeling, without being judgmental and blaming, and to own that. Approach her from a place of love, human to human. The next step was for S. to let the girl know that her need to be treated with respect was not being met and that she was very hurt.

S. was intrinsically able to empathize with the girl. She understood that this bully was simply calling out for love. This girl, who was much smaller then S., was essentially provoking and initiating a beat-down. Luckily, S. did not want to smash her. Instead, S. was able to see that this girl was looking for support from her peers, saying, "Look at me! I can make this big girl feel miserable." Likely, this bully felt like an outsider herself, and so seized upon an opportunity to create another outsider in S., in order to direct attention away from her and secure her place within the group.

But S. already knew all about feeling like an outsider and used this as a kind of secret power to neutralize the girl through Non-Violent Communication. S. knew that in her heart, this girl was simply suffering from low self-esteem, and S. could view the girl with empathy rather than fear. Not only was S. able to end the bullying, but the two girls became friends. S. reached out to her bully in honesty and respect, viewing her as a worthwhile fellow human being. By coming from a place of love, she was able to create an atmosphere where the bully could get what she was truly asking for: love.

Challenge

Cyber-bullying along with the traditional schoolyard taunting has created a cloud of intensity that seriously inhibits the learning process. Our culture of bullying and negative response has snowballed into countless behavioral outbursts, distractions and misguided imposition of consequences by school staff. Rarely does the bullying stop—this is because the person doing the bullying is simply labeled and further ostracized.

Even our best intentions sometimes backfire. Often, rather than addressing and resolving the bullying issue, teachers contribute to and exacerbate the problem by using judgmental, exclusionary language. This reflects how deeply ingrained a dualistic, materialistic paradigm has become in our culture.

The stakes are high, of course. Kids are losing their lives. This is terrifying and tragic. As parents, teachers and counselors, we are

41

afraid for our children and many of our solutions have sprung from a place of fear. We are doing the best we can with what we're given. But if we could simply slow down and look more deeply into the root of the bullying rather than just the aftermath, we will be able to minimize the collateral damage as a whole for all parties involved.

Those promoting the "zero-tolerance" and other "anti-bullying" programs believe they are working towards a more peaceful and safe solution. But these programs ultimately work to exclude and isolate the bully, making the situation more dangerous.

Goal

We need to stand back and recognize that there's another way of being in the world. We need to acknowledge and accept that our current path is becoming more problematic and divisive. This is especially true in our schools where young minds are being impressed with an intention to mold them into a desired likeness or image.

We need to recognize that we are all connected. When witnessing a situation where one student is bullying another, our first response is often to comfort the child we see as the victim. But we need to let ourselves feel equally connected to *both* children. Both children, in many ways, are victims. Both children need our help. We need to be able to be with each other in a way that is free of judgment and condemnation and, instead, full of understanding and acceptance of our inherent oneness.

Practical Application

Acceptance versus Ostracism

Many systems of problem resolution such as *Non-Violent Communication* and *Collaborative Problem Solving*[13] have evolved to offer practical ways to address the deficits of our current system. Generally, except where school systems have developed more innovative ways to address the issue of misconduct among students (such as those mentioned here), the methods used are more punitive in nature than restorative and rehabilitative. Typically, students are subjected to various forms of detention or suspension and minimal attempts are made to ascertain which are the complex dynamics motivating the behavior, such as psychological/emotional, and/or socio-economic circumstances. By integrating one or more of these innovative models into our schools, we may transform the classroom environment and greatly enhance the quality of education.

These modalities all have one thing in common: they focus on treating every individual with respect. There are no us versus them, nor Bully vs. Victim paradigms. We need to start rooting for everyone. "But you don't understand," some people might say. "This bully is beyond help. This bully is evil and hurtful and out of control. The only way to handle her is to set her apart from everyone to protect the other children."

There are two parts to consider about this situation.

The first question to ask: In whose best self-interest is it when you set one child apart from the rest? If we look deep inside ourselves, we will find that the answer is likely that it is best for *us*. Our classes are over-crowded, and even the best kids are high-maintenance. Isn't it easier to set the troublemakers apart so the rest can go about their business of learning and living? But singling a kid out as the bad guy doesn't solve the problem. Putting someone in a corner only strengthens their poor self-concept and helps them internalize that label, that message that *I'm the bad guy*. Some kids even get pleasure being the guy who can get so much attention by stirring up trouble. They simply don't know any other way, so they must be told and guided to the idea that there *is* another way. We need to get to a place where we can see that the bully needs our love just as much as the one being victimized. Imagine if we work to draw out the extraordinary wisdom and potential within the bully, as well as from the kid being bullied. By redirecting that bully's inappropriate actions, we will be able to add two phenomenal kids to our roster, instead of excising one.

The second consideration is: This is most likely not the first time this child has bullied. But what if it was? What if the very first time this child acted out in a way that we label *being a bully* someone responded to her in kindness instead of contempt? What if someone worked to bring her back into the fold instead of ostracizing her more? Often, teachers come into the new school year with stories about the troublemakers in the classroom. Repeat offenders aren't given the opportunity of a clean slate because we expect bad behavior from them—and so, we get it. But what if we say, "Okay, Billy is a bully, but let's look at his home life, how his parents treat him, and how we've treated him. He has progressed through school year after school year without any truly loving support." And then, what if we say, "That stops here."

We picture bullies in the classroom, but really, bullies exist throughout our lives, in all places and at all ages. So, although many of these examples are directed towards teachers, we can all integrate these ideas into our everyday practices.

Coping Mechanisms

Coping mechanisms need to be introduced and children encouraged to use them along with adolescents so that they can better navigate the many challenges they face at home, school or play. While working in the children's department at a counselling center, I attended a training program conducted by a psychologist who developed an exceptional treatment program for adolescents in the Baltimore area. One of the skill sets he promoted among his charges was "Stop, chill and choose!" The simple efficacy of this dictum is profound. Rather than the typical, impulsive, knee-jerk reactive response to unpleasant stimulus typical of both young and older people alike, "Stop, chill and choose!" entails a much more thoughtful and satisfyingly effective way of resolving conflict. As this strategy is employed, one remembers to create a gap of time between the stimulus and the response. During that gap, one may take a few slow, deep breaths and access one's poise and bearings with the intention to calm down, to be better able to focus upon the task at hand. After chilling out, one then becomes more able to examine the various options for responding and then, carefully, chooses the one which, hopefully, will invite the happiest resolution.

The Golden Rule

Another strategy which may enhance a child or adolescent's problem-solving repertoire is to emulate the wisdom of the Golden Rule. To truly apply the guidance of treating others as one would prefer to be treated requires an understanding of the spirit of the Namaste Principle – recognition that other and self are divine and therefore, need to be treated with the love and respect due such a presence. This suggests our need to hold *ourselves* in high esteem and therefore, worthy of kindness and respect. As we then consider how we are to treat others, we understand that the Golden Rule directs us to put aside our anger and condemnation in favor of kindness and respect.

A concern has arisen for me in a surprising observation I have made when asking many of the young people I counsel to define what is their understanding of the Golden Rule. Many of their faces present a blank stare, reflecting their ignorance of the concept! Not only does their level of comprehension of the concept range from vague to none at all, but they also seem unable to even grasp the concept when it is explained to them! Possibly, their young, impressionable minds are just waiting for parents and teachers to proactively present this concept in such a manner that they may integrate it into their consciousness.

A humorous and yet possibly, alarming sidebar to the Golden Rule issue arose when a particularly mischievous young man presented his understanding of the Golden Rule: "Do unto others before they do unto you!"

The Rooms

Those in the recovery community know what I mean when I say, *the rooms*. But for those who aren't versed in the lingo of addiction, the title of this section is referring to the rooms in which meetings are held—generally, Alcoholics Anonymous meetings, but for our purposes, the meeting rooms of any kind of addiction support group.

And regardless of whether or not you have visited the rooms officially, as an addict or as a family member of an addict, this chapter will likely have some relevance for your life. Given my own experience during a period of time in life when I felt deep dissatisfaction to the point of despair, turning to alcohol and marijuana to numb my emotional state, I know this is not unique yet a very human story, relevant to many of us or those close to us.

Story

Over forty years ago, I was doing steel mill shift work out in the Midwest. As one of the younger men and a newcomer, I had a work schedule that toggled between day and night shifts. There was no regularity or rhythm to my work schedule and my equanimity was thrown out of balance. I began drinking a lot in my off-hours, and this exacerbated a pattern of poor sleep issues. Yet I was young, and my mind and body were able to withstand and tolerate the abuse to which I was subjecting them. In fact, I even believed my method was working—I was unhappy with my daily labors, and the alcohol seemed to dull my despair. In reality, I was simply in denial.

A few years later, I was hired to be part of a coordinated team on an in-patient unit of a comprehensive community mental health center. We worked so closely together that we all partied after hours and yes, alcohol and marijuana were part of the partying. Also, I was working all three shifts again, filling in coverage gaps – an erratic schedule for me. I'd recently returned from my travels in India, and I was playing head games with myself that this was all facilitating my spiritual journey. Yet, there are risks and limitations to relying on such substances. I had just discovered Ram Dass's book *Be Here Now*[14] and was beginning to perceive my experience with psychedelics as a precursor to moving more deeply into a spiritual journey, just as Ram Dass had done. What I lacked at this time was the sort of guidance Ram Dass received from his guru, Neem Karoli Baba.

After a very eventful year of working at the in-patient unit, I attended a seminar on "Yoga and Psychotherapy" at a holistic health center. This not only provided me with a clear understanding of how I could integrate the concepts and practices of Eastern and Western thought, but I would soon encounter the quality of guidance that was so transformative for Ram Dass. Choosing to quit my job and become an ashramite under the head swami's direction at the yoga institute, I committed myself to an exceptional training program free of drugs, sex and rock 'n' roll.

Yet, I still had much to learn, as I transitioned back into the real world, life presented me with many lessons. Risë and I had become a couple. I resumed working in the mental health field and we were invited to move to the new headquarters of the yoga institute in another state.

Ironically, after spending several years studying and practicing yoga and meditation there, I found myself resorting again to alcohol instead of turning to spiritual practice to ease my dulled spirit. Soon,

I was attending grad school, starting a family, and working the night shift — again! The night shift was always my worst enemy. I felt like a zombie most of the time and was often running on caffeine and cigarettes. My schedule was such that I worked four days on, then, took two days off. I got into a pattern of drinking on my first night off. I always drank while doing chores—yardwork and housework mostly, so it was easy to tell myself drinking was not problematic because I wasn't in a bar and because I was only drinking one day a week.

But that one day of drinking spilled over into every other day. Even though I wasn't drinking every day, I was making myself miserable, and the pattern was especially distressing for my wife, Risë, who had to deal with the brunt of my moodiness. My anxiety and anger and irritability continued to get worse. My four-days-on-and-two-days-off schedule was wearing on all of us.

I'd been working at the facility for nine years when I met up with a friend, R., who'd begun working at a local treatment center. Risë had shared with R. some of her concerns about my drinking, and we had a deeply thoughtful discussion. His approach was incredibly interesting to me and included a holistic mission I believed in. R. told me I'd be great at the center, but that everyone who worked there had to be clean and sober for at least one year before he would hire them. I also happened to have one year left to work at my job in the mental health field in order to become fully vested in the retirement program. I had a year to make the change.

I resolved not to drink anymore at all. My daughter was about four years old by this time, and I had enough seniority to get day shift work instead of night shift, which allowed me a much more regular schedule. In order to help me battle the booze, I returned to my daily meditation practice and focused on a healthy diet. Within a month, I was able to achieve some of the same positive feelings I was seeking, but not finding, from drinking. This was a revelation for me. Once my state of mind and emotions were in balance again, and my priorities became clear as I took better care of myself, I experienced a natural "high" akin to what I was seeking to feel through substance abuse. This was a key factor in my transformation and revealed a new understanding — there is a way of moving into balance in one's life and really feeling joyful that can only happen when we are not using chemical or alcoholic substances. The fleeting happiness we feel with substances is false. The combination of a regular schedule and no toxicity in my body helped me achieve more in my personal meditation then I ever had before. I got out of the dysfunctional zombie routine, and I was able to achieve a deeper clarity. This was a revelation—I had found a state I could not achieve by drinking or smoking pot or anything. I was keeping my mind focused. I went to an open AA meeting with our friend, R. This is where I learned about the most important part of the Twelve Steps: surrender.[15]

When a person *hits bottom* he is ready for the rooms. Although the Twelve Step Program evolved out of addressing the hopelessness of alcoholism, the program is relevant for all forms of addiction. The process of joining anonymously with others facing the same challenges while devoting oneself to the Twelve Step Program, has opened countless people to a way of transcending addiction. Attending meetings in the ubiquitous rooms offers addicts a way of living in the world, yet not of it.

A room where the Twelve Step Program takes place may not technically exist as one of the rooms of our house, but the context of it so deeply addresses the intention of this book to align oneself with our shared, spiritual Beingness that the need to include it in our discussion becomes evident. Indeed, the urgency to address the enormous challenge that the world currently faces in attenuating the endemic addiction crisis is stunning. In a *New York Times* article dated June 18th, 2017, the following statistic was given: "Drug overdoses are now the leading cause of death among Americans under the age of 50."

Challenge

As human beings, we crave joy and success. When we're not connecting with these feelings, we feel anxiety and depression. Typically, then, we try to fill that hole of despair, as I had done and illustrated in the previous story. Like many others, instead of reaching inward to work at accessing the source of the deepest happiness of the true Self, I tried for a long time to fill my hole of despair seeking material things and immersing myself in external sources of fleeting happiness.

During my years of study at the yoga institute, I remember many concepts, practices and stories which I have woven into my life, both personally and professionally. A day does not pass without my drawing upon one or another aspect of the collective wisdom these teachings offer. The metaphorical element of stories told by spiritual teachers is something I have found particularly transformative. One of these stories identifies the nature of the challenge we encounter as we attempt to live in the world, yet not of it.

A master who had been guiding an especially serious and gifted student directed him to test his self-mastery skills. A mansion housing many rooms filled with all kinds of sensual delights such as wine, seductive women, food, and captivatingly beautiful art works, was to be the setting for the student's next challenge. The master directed that, while holding a goblet of wine filled to the brim, the student was to walk through each room in the mansion without spilling a drop of wine. Upon successful completion of this first task, the student was then told that he must repeat the same task yet, this time, he was to indulge himself in all the sensual delights of the rooms while still not allowing a drop of wine to spill from the brimming goblet that he would carry once again.

As we become aware of a deeper purpose in life and begin to embrace the wisdom of finding treasure in the depth of the spiritual heart, we are no longer satisfied with the mundane. We yearn for a higher experience. Lacking the sort of spiritual guidance offered by the spiritual master in the previous tale, many people are seduced into experiences which provide intense, but unenduring highs. Whether it is alcohol, drugs, sex, gambling or any number of other substances or behaviors which appear to offer an escape from the monotonous routine of daily living, the fallacy of their short-lived promise becomes apparent.

Addiction has grown exponentially, like an aggressive cancer. Our culture has lost its spiritual and moral foundation. There are trends occurring worldwide that appear to be contributing to and hastening the infectious spread of addiction. Religions have become less relevant as evidenced by decreasing membership over many years now. Paradoxically, religion has become central in much of the political and social unrest across the world. This trend coincides with an explosive increase in the sales of electronic devices and the ever-growing fascination with social media. Polarization in politics and all the divisiveness with which this entails has greatly increased levels of fear and anxiety.

The deterioration of the integrity of the family unit is a particularly alarming trend. Divorce rates, domestic abuse, and teen and adult crime rates, all on the rise, are some of the symptoms of the loss of our spiritual and moral foundation. A spiritual vacuum has been created which cultivates an environment in which the addictive mind is primed. The loss of simple emotional connection to one another has seduced us into addictive behaviors to relieve the uncertainty, resignation, anxiety and fear swirling all around us.

Every morning at the yoga institute, we would say a particular prayer in Sanskrit and then again in English, about cultivating the capacity to disarm fear, uncertainty and illusion. The inherent petition of the prayer was to evoke *viveka*, which means discernment or discrimination. This prayer told a story about walking through the forest and thinking about a fear of snakes. If fear of snakes is our focus, then we will see a snake in every movement on the floor of the forest. However, when we have clarity, we will see the truth—a rope on the ground is just a rope, not a snake. Prayer is about

51

strengthening our mind to become more discerning, and when we can see the rope instead of the serpent we see the reality instead of the illusion. In our human vulnerability and identifying with our fears, we see danger where there is none. When we can see the rope instead of the serpent, we stop seeing potential danger and enemies lurking about. Instead, we see people who are also fighting a hard battle in life. Instead of preparing ourselves for a counterattack because we are expecting to be attacked, we remain clear, calm, and peaceful.

Too often, we look to external resources such as drinking alcohol, taking drugs, eating, sex, gambling, or any number of other things to fill a hole that is inside of us. We look to addictions to soothe by making that hole disappear briefly. In the rooms, there is an old saying that goes: *Poor me, poor me, pour me another one.* All too often the dullness of spirit that we experience seeks relief in our external cravings which are never quite satiated. How can we fill the internal yearning for the deepest satisfaction at our spiritual core with superficialities? Disconnected from ourselves and others, we can't find the right key that will open the door to the storehouse of ever-abiding peace and happiness within the divine spark in our hearts waiting to be birthed into the light of our days.

The key is joyful connection—to the self/Self and to one another. Yet, each person's path to finding this connection will be different. The Rooms offer one approach—an approach that has worked for many. I first learned about *The Blue Book of Alcoholics Anonymous* from a security guard I knew at one of my jobs. He hardly ever drank, but when he did he went whole hog. He found his way to AA and became as fervent in spreading the AA word as if he were a born-again Christian. He worked to spread the word about AA, but most of the people on the night shift were drinkers and so they didn't want to hear what he had to say. The night shift routine was to simply stay awake in case someone got into a fight on the floor, so mostly we just sat and talked. I was very interested in what he had to say because the more I listened, the more I realized that what he was talking about was very close to what I'd been studying. We were on the same wave length but coming from different perspectives. Essentially, the Twelve Steps were much like the Eight Limbs of Raja Yoga, or like the Process of Inquiry of Ramana Maharshi's teachings, when taking the *fearless moral inventory* in the Twelve Steps Program.

Night shift duty can be tedious and so one night, I read through part of the Big Blue Book. I was struck by similarities between AA and the spiritual attunement and meditation practices I was learning about. I broke through my denial, which was a major stumbling block to my recovering from alcoholism. I knew that when I was in balance the peace and happiness came from within. The essence of the Twelve Steps is about becoming spiritually attuned to the recognition that when we try to use something external to fill a void within us, it is going to fail—only by going inward can we discover what we're looking for – lasting happiness and satisfaction.

However, the trick is maintaining that balance which comes from within our spiritual core.

Goal

The Namaste Principle is inherent within the Twelve Step model of self-transformation. As we commit to this model, we align ourselves with our shared divinity by engaging in the self-inquiry of a fearless moral inventory – Step Four. We engage in the process of awakening to our true spiritual nature through prayer and meditation – Step 11. We thus transcend our addictive thinking. All of this requires a willingness to do the work of self-examination and surrender to change. When the dead end of addiction is realized and the sense that *there must be another way* is not only possible but achievable, we are ready to begin the process of restoring balance and wholeness to our lives.

Practical Application

Mindfulness

Those familiar with the Twelve Step Program understand how important the phase of a fearless moral inventory is in the process of change. Each of us will benefit from some form of this method of self-examination. Plato's *Apology of Socrates* quotes: "The unexamined life is not worth living!" holds relevance here.[16] The question remains also for us: how may we best examine our lives? Essentially, this is about a kind of mind-training process. We need to witness the flow of our thoughts, statements and actions each day. To witness means that we pay attention to our judgmental thoughts and reactive emotions, while we also remain present to the momentary, passing activities of daily living. This is commonly defined as the practice of mindfulness.

Practicing mindfulness meditation leads naturally to meditation in action – acting, moving, and responding to life each moment with conscious attention to the emotions and mental judgements which motivate our behavior. This requires a detached Mr. Spock kind of objectivity -- not taking anything personally, not condemning nor evaluating -- just a clear, unbiased observation of what is. As we cultivate our discernment and our non-judgmental faculties, we will be able to recognize that some beliefs we hold are distorted and need to be clarified and adjusted while others are valid and perhaps need to be fortified.

Thus, a fearless moral inventory leads us into a deeper level of self-understanding. What arises from this process is an attitude which no longer condemns bad, evil, sinful behavior setting us at war with ourselves and others. Upon closer examination of how our behavior is shaped by our external and internal experiences, we might realize that we are doing the best we can with what we have been given from our historical conditioning in the form of familial, educational, social and economic upbringing. Such a realization blossoms into forgiveness – when we no longer condemn ourselves, we are freed to express the deep empathy and love at the core of our spiritual nature. Self-compassion and true empathy for others can arise. This realization, grounded in the spiritual truth of our Being, is what the spiritual awakening through prayer and meditation refers to in Step 11 of the Twelve Steps Program.

A Practice in How to Meditate

The practice of meditation is similar to playing a musical instrument or becoming skilled at an athletic sport. As a novice in playing music or sports, one is taught the fundamentals of playing, gradually building upon the fundamentals until one excels in one's playing to either play more challenging pieces of music or play competitively. Similarly, in the beginning, one is guided in basic preparation for meditation: finding a quiet place free from distractions and noise and sitting erect yet comfortably and choosing some form of concentration to use which allows a relaxation of physical, mental and emotional tension. Eventually, with repetition, one can graduate to meditate in action, that is, while one is carrying out one's daily activities, joyfully maintaining a relaxed, focused, clear state of awareness.

What I am about to describe to you is an integration of my training in the Raja Yoga tradition of meditation along with elements of the hypnotherapeutic induction process. After practicing meditation for over 15 years, I had been pleasantly surprised to discover during my training in hypnotherapy that the states arising from meditation practice or hypnotherapeutic induction are similar in the quality of natural balance to which one is restored via either process. The common key in either process is to stay present in the moment such that a way is opened to begin unravelling the stress of complex, daily living which takes its toll in physical, mental and emotional tensions that grow eventually from dis-ease to disease.

Let's begin the steps as mentioned previously in preparation for this state of natural balance to emerge. Set aside an appointed time and place each day, free from distractions and noise as much as possible, where you can sit comfortably on a sturdy chair or cushion. Make sure your head, neck and spine are held gently yet firmly erect while resting your hands in your lap or on your knees with palms soft and fingers softly curled in a relaxed manner. While remaining aware of holding yourself in a comfortable, upright position, expand your awareness to scan the body from head to toe, consciously relaxing any areas of discomfort by softening the skin, muscles or bones in each of those areas, one area at a time. Now, focus your eyes upon a point in front of you, which can be the flame of a burning candle or a spot on the wall. Take a few moments to see what you see without shifting your focus from that point. Then, keeping your eyes fixed on the candle flame or point, notice the sounds around you, outside the room, within the room – even the sound of your own breath breathing itself through you, in and out. Now, become aware of your tactile sense: feel your hands, the weight of your body settling onto the seat and the floor, the movement in your chest and belly as your breath flows in and out. Maybe you can even notice the subtle shifting temperature within your nostrils – a slight cooling sensation as you breathe in, and a slight warming as you breathe out. Simply notice what you are sensing as you turn your attention to sounds, physical sensations and any thoughts or feelings as they arise.

Then, while continuing to notice what you hear, see or feel, direct your attention in an even more focused way to your breath. Prepare to take three deep breaths, holding each in-breath a few moments before slowly exhaling: possibly counting to 3 mentally on the in-breath and counting to 6 mentally on the out-breath to enhance concentration. After a gentle inhalation, breathe out fully as if you are squeezing all the air out of your lungs. Then, slowly fill your lungs to capacity and hold this inhalation a few moments before exhaling slowly again. On the third breath, hold the inhalation a little longer, if possible. Then, as you slowly breathe out, let your eyes relax their focus closing gently and allow your breath to return to its natural rhythm and tone. Be present to how the breath is breathing you: you are being breathed.

Now, let your awareness travel slowly from head to toe observing once again each part of your body while letting tightness and discomfort fall away with each breath. The gentle rhythm of your breath will deepen this falling away: feel the belly gently expanding with each in-breath and contracting with each outbreath. As your awareness reaches your feet and toes, take a moment to feel the comfort of your whole body as you give your mind permission to also let go of any worrisome concerns about the past or the future. Returning your attention to your breath, begin listening inwardly to the sound "So" as you breathe in and the sound "Hum" as you breathe out. Keep in mind the message of this "So Hum" mantra: "" I am (So) That (Hum), reminding us of our true nature, that is, we are not human beings having a spiritual experience, but spiritual beings having a human experience. This mantra message parallels Step 11 in the Twelve Step Program[17] where awakening is referred to as that shift in our consciousness in which we remember that *I am not this limited, vulnerable being; I am Spirit – eternal, invulnerable.*

Keeping our intention to focus the mind upon breath and mantra, we might notice a flow of thoughts, memories, sensations and fantasies that arise in our awareness. Our task while sitting is to observe these impressions as a witness and then return to focus upon breath and mantra. Witnessing entails observing without evaluating or judging, that is, not identifying in some emotional way with the impressions arising in our awareness. Of course, some of the impressions which arise as we sit in meditation will trigger emotions. Again, the key is to remain present, remembering that the past is over and cannot be changed, while the future can only be imagined. So, as emotions arise while we practice meditation, we cultivate the capacity to observe the drama of those emotions as if they were a movie. Then we return to the breath and mantra as an anchor for letting go into one-pointed stillness.

As the mind becomes more skilled at witnessing the array of impressions which arise as we meditate, we naturally extend that same mindfulness to our daily activities. We are then practicing meditation in action.

The Backyard

Story

Often, as Risë and I are enjoying the glorious expanse of landscape surrounding us (even while we're on vacation visiting some forest, mountain, river or ocean shoreline), I'll say: "This is our backyard!" This statement may seem silly or maybe even arrogant, but my perspective in saying this is not that we own what we're viewing but that no matter who or where we are, we share in the privilege of enjoying the majesty and beauty of this planet. Along with the privilege of enjoying the planet's bounty comes also the responsibility of stewardship: doing all we can to regain the balance of nature that has been lost in our selfish taking from the earth without giving back to it or preserving its diverse forms of life – animal, human, mineral, plant, and waters all.

As I was growing up in the Midwest, August was our family's time to load up the car with our camping gear and head for the hills. My parents, three sisters, and I would follow my mother's carefully planned itinerary, staying in campgrounds all across the country. We visited many of the national parks, from Acadia to Yellowstone, creating a treasure of memories for each of us, as well as a deep appreciation for the seemingly limitless expanse of our backyard.

My sense of the world being a backyard for all beings who dwell upon it deepened as I later travelled on my own to Europe and overland to India. The blurring of boundaries and the dubious concept of territorial ownership were becoming more evident to me as I experienced the deeper quality of what living on this planet was really all about. The arbitrary, ego-driven division of regions into separate cities, states, countries and even empires, has created circumstances that ignore or deny the reality that the human race has evolved from the same source: we're all One People!

Aboriginal cultures across the planet, who generally have maintained a harmonious connection with the rhythms and cycles of nature, have a deep appreciation, care and respect for the land they inhabit. Chief Seattle spoke of the web-like nature of all of life: whatever happens to one tiny part of the web affects the entire web. Another Native American perspective to highlight is the Seventh Generation directive: whatever we do now to the land, water and air, we do so mindful of the effect that this will have not only in the present moment or near future, but upon the seven generations of those beings who will follow us.

During my freshman year at Elmhurst College in 1970, the first Earth Day was observed and during this time, the Elmhurst Administration was very proactive in raising our consciousness regarding environmental issues and concerns. Paul Ehrlich and Ralph Nader were among the speakers invited to prompt us to consider our role in preserving the integrity of our planet. It was an exciting, albeit distressing time. People all over the world were engaged in a way of looking at the damage human culture had done to the planet. The Old Testament biblical directive found in Genesis 1:26 that man should have dominion over the earth and all its inhabitants could be viewed then and now, from a distorted perspective: coloring and shaping a prevalent paradigm of fear-based thinking in which human domination over the earth's resources without respectful stewardship of those resources has devastating results! Earth Day, celebrated every year since then, has been an opportunity to focus upon awakening each of us to rightful stewardship of the earth so as to reverse, or at the least, diminish these destructive trends.

The Namaste Principle offers a way to reframe our perspective toward our planet as well as toward all its inhabitants. Many people have begun to recognize the living, even spiritual nature of this amazing planet. Some people refer to it as Gaia. Contemporary ecological theory has drawn this mythical name from ancient Greece: Gaia, ancestral mother of all life, the primal Mother Earth Goddess. The term was revived in 1979 by James Lovelock in *Gaia: A New Look at Life on Earth*, which hypothesizes that living organisms and inorganic material are part of a dynamic system which shapes the earth's biosphere, and maintains the Earth as a fit environment for life. This is where the greeting "Namaste!" can be addressed to not only our fellow human beings, but to all creatures, great and small, and to the very earth itself.

Challenge

An imperative we now face in our relationship to the earth, particularly for Western cultures, more than any we have so far discussed, is this: fear-based materialism, fueled by an interpretation of the Old Testament dictum about man's dominion over the earth that is skewed by selfish interest in conquest and greed, has left humanity and the planet, in a pickle, as the saying goes. Endless wars and the seemingly insatiable pursuit of more and more possessions which are the latest vogue, have so depleted or destroyed our natural resources that we may soon find ourselves on a planet which can no longer sustain us for the long term.

Goal

Shifting our perspective toward honoring the inherent divinity of all beings and living things will inevitably alter and enhance the manner in which we take care of our backyard, whether it is our individual backyard or the larger earth backyard. As each one of us chooses to be more proactive in our relationship with the earth and the parts of the planet that we touch in our small corners of the world, staying grounded in the Namaste Principle, our Mother Earth/Gaia will slowly return to balance.

The evolution of the human brain has given us an extraordinary selection of diverse freedoms. We have visited the moon; created the global internet; transplanted hearts and even created life in vitro – just a few of the wondrous expressions of human discovery, invention and creativity. However, with freedom comes responsibility. The universal law of *karma* always determines that when there's an error or imbalance in our ability to be responsible – that is, responding with integrity in any given situation – there will be a loss of freedom. For example, a simple metaphor to illustrate this is the phenomenon of fire: when using a source of fire with caution and care, fire will cook our food and keep us warm when needed; when we lack mindfulness in utilizing fire, it can destroy us.

To the degree that our global culture awakens to the divinity we share with all of life, we will experience harmony with our planet and with one another. An old friend of mine used to quote this adage: "The world is a banquet and most poor bastards are starving to death."[18] The tragic validity of this commentary as it applies to our past may be refuted as we shift away from a fear-based materialistic paradigm to a spiritual paradigm grounded in respect and love. The choice is ours.

Practical Application

Tending garden

Even if you live in an apartment with no yard, you might want to explore how to bring nature from the outside into your interior space —possibly, using potted plants to decorate and breathe oxygen into living quarters; maybe even creating a terrarium or growing sprouts from alfalfa seeds for salad. If you do have a yard, research how it might be a habitat for other species: it's all god, all good. You may want to consider refraining from using commercial fertilizers and chemicals and enrich and replenish the soil with compost by using plant-based table scraps. This is a way to give back to the natural environment. See how you might find plant species compatible with your climatic conditions or those which are found growing wild in your locale, incorporating them into your landscape. Which plants support each other side by side in your living space? Keep a balance—make it easy on yourself to only plant that which you can maintain without undue effort. Share your bounty with neighbors and family or even a local soup kitchen. Mindfulness can be applied even here: the whole process of gardening might be viewed as a metaphor for so many areas of our life: slowly and steadily tending the garden – mulching, weeding, watering and keeping pesky critters out of the garden will reap a lush harvest!

Staying Informed

In honoring that others' lives are connected to one's own, you could cultivate an understanding of global trends in environmental and climate issues; commercial farming and fishing; local and international government regulations or lack thereof; and follow the work of environmentally friendly charities. Maybe you can support them in whatever way works for you via membership or reading their newsletters and magazines. The planetary backyard is larger than your small spot of land! Maybe being an activist resonates with you, so you may want to participate in local environmental groups. Remember that the Namaste Principle is grounded in the principle of the unity of all living things—not just human, but the entire cosmos. John Muir noted that: "When we try to pick out anything by itself, we find it hitched to everything else in the Universe."[19]

Networking

If you enjoy connecting with others socially, reach out to others in friendship or in civic responsibility, and express your environmental concerns: encourage a dialogue of shared wisdom. Try using nonviolent communication to foster good relationships, easing stress and reducing isolation by owning your feelings, and affirming your needs and preferences: those people with differing or oppositional perspectives deserve your respect just as you would like to be heard respectfully. Seriously, consider that we're all in this life together even though each of us is a unique creation/individual. While others might be totally opposed to what you are saying, consider that divisive and polarizing dialogue creates alienation among people. Find your voice: one way might be to let it be heard by contacting your local and state government representatives to voice your views about your interests and concerns.

Enjoy and Explore the Natural World

Travel out of your house into the natural world around you as often as possible: hike, bike, and swim, kayak, daily or weekly, alone or with groups who join together in these activities. Take vacations to state or national parks, even other parts of the world. What wondrous discoveries await you! Yet, remember that travelling by air, sea or ground transportation pollutes the environment, so do whatever you can reasonably do to reduce the toll of fossil fuel wastes on the planet by reducing your carbon footprint. While travelling, engage with those you meet with the Namaste Principle in the forefront of your interactions and it will enrich the quality of your communication and possibly foster a greater sense of togetherness in the world.

Tipping Point: Which Way to Choose?

Over the course of human history, there have been significant changes in the way we have viewed the primary realities that shape how we interact with each other. The capacity to use fire to cook food and warm our dwelling places; the invention of the wheel to transport material and people; the capacity to plant, cultivate and harvest crops for food – these are just a few of the discoveries which have radically transformed the lifestyle of our ancestors to that of our contemporaries. Gradually, in time, subtler, that is, more sophisticated innovations arose: mathematics, astronomy, language, the arts, sciences and militarization each, in countless ways, ushered in extraordinary changes in the ways we thought, spoke and acted.

The term *paradigm shift* (which may loosely apply to the previously mentioned changes occurring throughout history) was identified by American physicist/philosopher, Thomas Kuhn (1922-1996). He defined a paradigm shift as a fundamental change in the basic concepts and experimental practices of a scientific discipline.[20] Kuhn applied the paradigm shift concept to a range of social and natural science phenomena. In the natural sciences, he observed the transition in cosmology that occurred in 1543 from Ptolemaic cosmology to a Copernican model; and in 1859, the transition in evolutionary theory from goal-directed change to Charles Darwin's natural selection was revolutionary. Furthermore, in 1920, another paradigm shift arose with a moving away from the worldview of Newtonian physics to the relativism of an Einsteinian worldview. Typically, paradigm shifts have been met with great resistance (Copernicus was nearly burned at the stake!) but ultimately, these shifts have become grounded in popular acceptance.

Malcolm Gladwell is a contemporary journalist and author of several bestselling books including *The Tipping Point* in which he asserts that changes in our culture often arise very much as a disease moves through a population.[21] As a reporter for the *Washington Post* in the 1980s, Gladwell discovered that the term *tipping point* was used in epidemiology to describe how, once a virus reaches a critical mass of infection, it quickly spreads throughout a wide cross-section of a population. Gladwell found that ideas can be as contagious as a virus. In the South Pacific area of Polynesia during the seventies and eighties, there was a phenomenon of teenagers committing suicide at a rate 10 times higher than anywhere else in the world. It was as though teens were infected with a suicide virus – each one killing themselves in exactly the same way under exactly the same circumstances. Gladwell suggests that any number of innovative ideas, products, and behaviors may infiltrate a population just as a contagious disease will. He is quick to say this is not a metaphor but a literal analogy.

Now, let's get back to The Namaste Principle and consider how this discussion of fundamental cultural change, paradigm shifts, and the tipping point may apply to what our present paradigm is all about and where a paradigm grounded in The Namaste Principle would lead us. The dominant paradigm of our planet has deep roots and arguably stretches back many millennia. What I am referring to here is the broadest and most general description of societal consciousness – a consciousness which is reflected in the minds of most people on planet Earth.

Of course, such generalizations fail to account for many

individuals and groupings of people who have certainly demonstrated a mindset quite other than the norm which I am suggesting has predominated for thousands of years.

The distinctive elements of the dominant world paradigm are:

1) A belief in one's material nature along with identification with the same (i.e. body, personality, intellect, possessions, roles, relationships) and

2) A thought system guided by fear in that all that defines one's self is vulnerable and subject to change, death and decay and therefore, must be defended against potential attack and extinction.

These two qualities dominating the worldview have been the source of wars, poverty and all kinds of strife. On the other hand, The Namaste Principle draws from a foundational viewpoint that is a place of strength and abundance yet allows compassion for our human tendency to fear and domination, while not identifying with the latter tendency. Rather than identifying with our limited, vulnerable material nature, we awaken to our eternal, invulnerable spiritual nature. As the viral nature of such an idea reaches the tipping point, we may find our world culture guided by a paradigm whose distinctive elements are:

1) A belief in the oneness of all beings and

2) A thought system guided by love and empathy in that we all share the same essence, the same pursuit of happiness, which ultimately resides in a return to the awareness of our divine source of being.

I am certainly not suggesting that, following this fundamental paradigm shift, that the world will be free of all suffering and violence, hatred and greed. No, as long as we inhabit human form and cling to our egos, we will be sucked back into much of the same kind of drama as history shows us. What we might look forward to, however, is a kinder world, in which we lean toward responding to its challenges, individually and globally, with a more consistently loving response rather than with fear and defensiveness.

A utopian world where peace and harmony reign for all will never exist. From *A Course in Miracles'* perspective, striving for such a perfect world would be an attempt "to make the error real"[22]and would be an exercise in futility. *A Course in Miracles* guides us to see the circumstances of our life as a classroom where we can transcend the battleground perspective. Each of us has within us both thought and emotional orientations, that of fear/ego and that of love/Spirit. The question is: Which one do we choose? This determines the quality of the life that we lead. As we become more consistently present in the classroom, we will find it more and more natural to perceive the presence of divinity within ourselves and within everyone we meet. As Pierre Teilhard de Chardin said: "We're not human beings having a spiritual experience, we're spiritual beings having a human experience."[23]

Waking up to this perspective is challenging work, requiring much self-reflection and self-adjustment. The more we engage in the work, the more we experience its joyful fruits. Even if the world persists in its tenacious grip on the dominant paradigm of materialism, of fear, each of us as individuals may choose to experience the peace that surpasses all understanding.

Which do you choose? Can you see the difference when you choose to respond with love rather than with fear and defensiveness? What are the fruits of your choices? Which world do you give to yourself and to others?

Looking Back from the Future

The Namaste Principle is not new – in fact, it is part of a revolutionary/ evolutionary movement toward self-transformation and hence, the transformation of the world, that has been going on since the beginning of time. *Living the Namaste Principle* is about engaging in a *way of being* that expresses a deep understanding of our eternal spiritual nature. It draws from the wisdom of the masters whose guidance across all cultures is that aligning our will and intention with our *identity as Spirit* will engender true happiness and peace. There are many paths that may guide us toward this way of being. Although the expressions or forms of each path may vary, there may be found an essential congruency that offers a common, unifying theme, one that directs the seeker to the goal of what is referred to in the New Testament as "the peace of God which surpasses all understanding."[24]

Just as we may reach the summit of Mt. Everest by choosing one of many paths or methods, we may awaken to the truth of *Being* by choosing the approach that best suits our sensibilities. The *essential congruency* referred to previously may be observed as a kind of touchstone which reveals the purity or truth of the path under exploration. In my experience, the qualitative state we are looking for is, most simply, love. In entering this state, people often find peace, or truth, or self-realization, or God – just some of the names by which people aim to define the essence of their experience.

Does the message of the path engender empathy and compassion toward others? Does it promote mutual understanding and respect toward all of life? Is there an experience of connecting with those around us that reflects a deepening of psychological, emotional and spiritual resonance? When these qualities are experienced as a direct outcome of the engagement of a path's guidance, one may be certain one is on *the right path*.

Victor Frankl, in *Man's Search for Meaning*, identified an innate yearning each of us possesses.[25] Some of us attend to the call of that inner voice more proactively than others, yet it is always there, offering a sort of North Star compass that leads us to the Mt. Everest of inner peace. The more we invest in the process of searching for that deeper sense of meaning, the more we begin to realize it is not an easy journey.

We are born into a family and a culture that has become aligned with a particular set of guidelines – religious, philosophical, political and socio-economic perspectives that offer a status quo that, generally, provide a sense of comfort and increasing familiarity. For many, that status quo is quite acceptable and following in the footsteps of the familiar works fine. For some people, however, contradictions, inconsistencies and the experience of cognitive dissonance prompts a questioning of the norm and a quest for Truth begins.

As for myself, I found the status quo to be full of holes. The family I was born into provided many comforts and opportunities. Perhaps what was most significant was the freedom I enjoyed following my questioning mind to refute the dogma of formal religion. Eventually, I discovered the universal truth within the various spiritual, philosophical, psychological and scientific approaches to understanding life to which my inquiry led me. My inner touchstone helped me discern the presence of this truth in the following systems which I have found to be inspired, inspiring and practical: from the Judeo-Christian tradition to Hinduism and Buddhism.

Your journey to discover the way of living out the Namaste Principle will be distinctly unique and different from mine. Perhaps, though, it will include some of the systems I have found so helpful; inevitably our paths to the Namaste Principle will be quite compatible.

My introduction to the Judeo-Christian tradition was through my family church. My father was a minister who preached the social gospel and was ecumenically oriented. His gentle manner allowed me to absorb the Christian message of forgiveness and inclusiveness and my father did not resist my questioning of the very existence of God. So, even as an avowed atheist, I was an active participant in the church community until I graduated from high school.

It was then that I began studying Eastern systems from the *Bhagavad Gita* and the *Upanishads* in the Hindu tradition to the *Tao Te Ching* and Zen Buddhism. What these texts taught me was that there is a way of engaging in spirituality very simply – without the rigidity of dogma I found to be so unacceptable in certain branches of Christianity. In fact, I was beginning to recognize that my inner touchstone was kicking in and I was connecting with how the essential message of Eastern thought is precisely what Jesus taught. I realized I wasn't an atheist after all. I had reframed the picture. My father had sensed that my "straying from the path" would ultimately lead me to the truth found in religion, in fact, in all religions -- and it did. I would never buy into the dogmatic structure of formal religion, but the path of spirituality has become my primary focus.

The journey to my spiritual Everest has been one upon which I've taken detours which seemed random, yet in retrospect, were quite synchronistic. In fact, I have long since learned that the unexpected moments of doubt and uncertainty are times to say "yes" and surrender to the adventure that inevitably follows. This capacity to surrender is part of the perspective my circuitous route to the Namaste Principle has taught me.

Growing up in the family of a Methodist minister offered me a way to get grounded in the Christian perspective without being indoctrinated in the "fire and brimstone" of sin, guilt and fear so common in many denominations. A unique dimension of my parents' perspective was how they met at a Unitarian gathering place in Boston where my mother had grown up – her parents were students of the Theosophical Society. My father was attending Divinity School at Boston University. The ecumenical perspective my parents possessed instilled within me an understanding that the differences each of us chooses regarding a spiritual path does not necessitate an exclusion or condemnation of others who happen to choose another path.

Perhaps my parents' tone of embracing all people despite their differences allowed me to remain engaged in the constructs of the church through my teen years, even though I considered myself to be an atheist. My quest to make sense of the world around me led me to reject the many un-scientific concepts which I saw in the Bible. So, for me, it seemed that the need to believe in God was based upon an unquestioning acceptance of ancient, superstitious beliefs and traditions. I also concluded that those who believe in God are unable to accept the fact that we only exist on this planet because it happens to be just the right distance from the sun to allow the natural process of evolution to have, over billions of years, brought us to our present state. I saw nothing divine about the creation of life, just a happy accident.

So, there I was – a teenager going through the motions of life, attending church and youth fellowship meetings. On the surface, I was playing the game like everybody else but underneath, I was trying to connect the dots and make sense of the rather mind-boggling complexities of what we call *life*. I saw no need to rebel and take a stance against religion. Unlike so many of the kids today, I ate whatever was put on my plate. When I found the piece of liver to be disgusting, I doused it with Worcestershire sauce and pepper, and ate it. What I found indigestible about religion could be overlooked when I found the experience of church services, Sunday School and youth fellowship to be rather interesting, and even at times, fun!

I reached a turning point at age 18 when I began reading material from the Eastern wisdom traditions. The *Bhagavad Gita* and the *Upanishads* – both classical Indian spiritual texts -- and *Zen Buddhism* by D.T. Suzuki introduced me to a whole new way of framing the picture of life. I was only beginning to wrap my mind around concepts that would take me decades to more fully understand and appreciate. The essential message of these texts resonated for me: there was a wisdom that felt so right, I was drawn to stay with it to go deeper. I also realized that the same message from the East was what the teachings of Jesus are truly guiding us to and not the rigid dogma of formal religion so often applied hypercritically to human behavior, leaving people confused, frustrated and alienated. Simply put, the teachings of the East and the teachings of Jesus lead us to learn to love all and exclude none because we're all one with God.

The purity of this message of unity, though, did not become clear to me for many years to come. I had much work to do. With some elaboration upon the details of my life journey, I will highlight the landmarks and describe how certain concepts and systems of thought came to me, along with an overview of what they offer.

It was the summer of 1969, after graduating high school that I stepped into the world of Eastern thought. As I entered college in the fall, other doors began opening for me: a curriculum which was partially focused upon critical thinking, cultural relativity and appreciation of deeper ways of relating to our world; the perspectives of other students from across the country -- some of whom had been to Woodstock -- and a few from around the world; and the extraordinary musical culture of the era. Another door – into the world of psychedelics – also opened for me and set me on a journey into inner space. Years later, I would discover that the practice of meditation is a more grounded, authentic path to understanding inner space, accessing and utilizing the powers of the mind beyond the ordinary.

After one and a half years of college, I decided to pursue other avenues of finding my place in the world. I had found that academia wasn't feeding my soul. The books I found enthralling were those I chose outside of the required reading of my classes. The works of Hermann Hesse, Fyodor Dostoevsky, Lao Tzu, Kurt Vonnegut, Paramahansa Yogananda, Aldous Huxley and others kept bringing me back to my existential quest. So, I left the formal education game and embarked on what would become several years' long patterns of working at a job while carrying on with my various interests and living independently. After a year or so, I set off for travels until my savings were gone and then found another job, worked a year and then traveled again. The quality of education I received while working as a medical orderly, physical therapy aide, steelworker, psychiatric technician in a mental health inpatient unit, and between jobs, hitchhiking cross country several times and flying to Europe and then, overland through Turkey, Iran, Afghanistan, and Pakistan to India and Nepal and then back to Europe and the States, was an education beyond anything I could have learned sitting in a classroom!

Now, regarding the various systems of thought that so transformed my perspective, and how they appeared in my life, it was as I journeyed overland back from India that I realized I needed to begin putting into practice what I was reading. The three months I spent in India had such a profound effect upon me – I realized the depth of what I was encountering in the Indian culture reflected thousands of years of applying the teachings of yoga and meditation to daily living, contributing to a complex and fascinating national history. For me to incorporate even a tiny fraction of what that was about I needed to start *practicing* – not just reading books about it. After my trip to India while I was working on a psychiatric inpatient unit, I began to find books that seemed to integrate the wisdom sources I'd been studying into practical applications for my life.

So, there I was, hired by a psychiatrist from the big city to establish a comprehensive community mental health center. The psychiatrist, who liked to be referred to as "Good King Edwin," hired his staff not based so much upon educational credentials, but upon the capacity to connect compassionately with the patients. We had engaged in a wide range of responsibilities inclusive of conducting group therapy, individual and family work. We had extensive guidance and ample opportunities to delve deeply into our inner resources.

In addition to this challenging work setting, I discovered while browsing in a bookstore Ken Keyes' *Handbook to Higher Consciousness* which I devoured. I memorized the Twelve Pathways which Keyes developed, went over them in my mind as I walked two miles to work every day, integrating them into my way of relating to everyone in my life. I then attended a three-day workshop Keyes led in the big city and learned how to strengthen this regimen. Keyes had taken many of the systems I'd studied – Patanjali's *Yoga Sutras*, Buddha's *Four Noble Truths*, Lao Tzu's *Tao Te Ching*, humanistic psychology, the teachings of Jesus and others, and synthesized the essence of each into his handbook. It offered me an ideal path for transformation and I eagerly ran down it.

One of the nurses I was working with turned me on to Baba Ram Dass' *Be Here Now* in which Ram Dass presents his own journey to the East and offers practical guidelines to seekers like myself, who want to integrate the practical wisdom of yoga into their lives. It was especially helpful as I was beginning the practice of hatha yoga with PBS TV's Lilias Folan who gently directed me into the basic postures and breathing exercises. Ram Dass offered a more expansive view of yogic practices including work with mantra. Months before, I had begun repeating a phrase presented by Ken Keyes who, rather than using terms that might seem foreign, referred to it as a "catalyst" (a mantra by any other name is still a mantra). "All ways us living love" ran through my mind while I walked – after I remembered the Twelve Pathways from his book, *Handbook to Higher Consciousness*.[26] Thanks to Ram Dass, I added "Om Mani Padme Hum", a Tibetan Buddhist mantra that frequently arises in my mind to this day, for which there is no easy translation into a simple phrase or sentence.

Loosely translated from reading Ram Dass' book *Be Here Now*, "Om Mani Padme Hum" means this: *Om* – the sum total of all energy, the first cause and the all-pervading sound; *Mani* means a jewel-like discrimination; *Padme* means lotus and *Hum* means heart. Personally, in my own mind, I considered it this way: an integration of the presence of divinity residing in my heart like a flowering lotus.

What I found so fascinating at this time was how my own inner journey into the world of consciousness expansion coincided with the real life encounters I was facing at my job. I saw how I could incorporate many of my newly-found insights into the process of addressing the challenges faced by the patients on the unit. The tools I used to facilitate my own growth could be translated into ways of assisting those under my care. I saw the possibility for them to achieve the same sort of self-awareness and self-control which I began to enjoy. What I was engaging in was still very much a "work in progress." All I knew at the time was that I was where I needed to be. The connection I felt with the patients, the staff (the quality of the relationship we had with each other was like that of family) and with myself was getting pretty deep!

Then, something very interesting happened. Good King Edwin passed on a brochure to me – one he had just received, and presumably, had not even examined. Once he saw it was about yoga and meditation, he gave it to me, knowing I was "into that crazy stuff" as he so playfully put it. The brochure announced a workshop for counselors and therapists designed to integrate yoga and meditation into psychotherapy. Of course, I signed up and was so impressed by what I experienced at the workshop that I quit my job and returned to the site of the workshop – the world headquarters of the yoga institute. There, I immersed myself in, not only the practice of Raja Yoga, but its practical application in a therapeutic setting.

The following year was a time of deep soul work for me. I had made a commitment to myself that I would adhere to the lifestyle of an ashram under the guidance of the swami whom I recognized as my Guru. His guidance reached beyond words. Once I worked through my initial resistance (this was not someone who fit my image of a meek, egoless teacher who would quietly guide me to enlightenment!), I came to terms with how I needed someone who would sternly direct me toward a more disciplined lifestyle. The power of Swamiji's loving presence was like nothing I had ever experienced! Moreover, his uncanny wisdom in directing me to take on tasks in which I lacked the self-confidence even to consider instilled within me a deep sense of trust.

Decades later, I now appreciate how that sense of trust was not about a person – it was about a trust in that *Beingness* that unites us all. Back then, though, I was simply surrendering to the flow of what each day offered me. The routine followed by the twelve to fourteen "boys" and the ten to twelve "girls" (to whom we were affectionately referred by Swamiji as we were all in our early 20's) was designed by him and provided us with an ideal lifestyle in which we had the opportunity to integrate the concepts and practices of Raja Yoga and Advaita Vedanta into our lives.

Waking at 5 a.m., we began each day with hatha yoga practice, followed by morning prayers (repeating traditional Hindu prayers in Sanskrit, then in English) and sitting meditation. This was followed by *karma yoga* (service), each of us engaging in our work assignments until breakfast at 10 a.m., a meal prepared by two of us. We had weekly shifts, so all of us had an opportunity to learn how to cook for a small group. The "girls" lived and ate in separate quarters. All returned to their karma yoga duties after breakfast and then had our main meal, dinner, at 4:30 p.m. There followed the fulfillment of more karma yoga responsibilities until evening when there was the option to either attend or teach hatha yoga classes for the public or listen to lectures by institute presenters or guest speakers. We also had the opportunity to attend most of the weekend seminars.

Swamiji's guidance throughout this process was remarkable. He met regularly with the "boys" and the "girls" (again, separately) to check in with how we were attending to our various tasks. He encouraged, praised and scolded as needed – all the while conveying his loving concern for each of us. Often, Swamiji would call to us individually: "Sonny!" and would then direct us in very specific ways. For example, once, as I was sitting alone in the library/meditation room where I was cataloguing the boxes of books donated for the graduate school program, he sat on the floor with me to talk. He proceeded, with no prompting on my part, to suggest how I might deal with the three issues with which I was struggling at that time. Having heard many similar accounts about and by Swamiji, I was not surprised that he could tune into another's mind as he did so deftly with mine that day on the floor. When he left, and I was alone to ponder his directives, I was nonetheless blown away by the powerful impact of such a penetrating presence!

In addition to my library task, Swamiji had assigned me to work as one of the assistants to the residential, holistic health program. After morning prayers, I would guide the five to seven residents attending the ten-day program in a gentle yoga class and again, later in the afternoon utilizing a different modality for enhanced self-awareness and well-being. In those afternoon sessions, I would monitor each of them in biofeedback training, and support them to stay on schedule with their other therapeutic activities. Each element of what I was absorbing through the multi-faceted experiences I underwent as an ashramite, was like a seed planted in rich soil. The holistic lifestyle shared in a community of like-minded seekers under the guidance of such a dynamic teacher as Swamiji, became a garden, the fruits of which I continue to harvest to this day.

For example, the process of integrating the concept and practices of Raja Yoga into my life has become the foundation of what I now call the Namaste Principle. While I learned the gentle, systematic way in which Swamiji led us to do the physical postures (*asana*) and breath awareness known to most people as yoga, I was simultaneously encouraged to understand the more subtle, true meaning of yoga. The asana and breath practices were but preparation for accessing the deeper meaning of yoga.

The term yoga derived from the Sanskrit word "yuj" which means to yoke, bind, or join, conveying the state of consciousness in which the individual, egotistical self awakens to and merges with the cosmic Self -- absolute, eternal reality. The eight limbs or rungs of Raja (or *Ashtanga*) Yoga comprise a systematic self-training program encompassing a way of cultivating a mindset and general way of being which is grounded in non-violence (*ahimsa*). *Ahimsa* is the first of the *yamas* (restraints) and is followed by nine other principles: *satya* (truthfulness), *asteya* (non-stealing), *brahmacharya* (balanced control of the senses), *aparigraha* (non-possessiveness), *shaucha* (purity), *santosha* (contentment), *tapas* (disciplined austerity), *svadhyaya* (self-study) *and Ishvara Pranidhana* (surrender to the Infinite, i.e. "Let go, let God!").[27] I like to refer to the *yamas* and *niyamas* as the 10 commitments which arise from being introspective of one's own thoughts, feelings and behavior, examining these to see if they are aligned with the ideals and virtues of the *yamas* and *niyamas*; and then truing up one's ongoing behavior to be in accord with these ideals. I was never comfortable with the Old Testament imposition of the 10 Commandments, yet these commitments spoke to my mind and heart with a lively resonance.

Something else I chose to commit to during my ashram days was a practice called *purush charana* – the repetition of the Gayatri Mantra 125,000 times. Using a *rudraksha mala,* which is like a rosary, I would say this mantra as I shifted each of the 108 beads with my middle and ring fingers and thumb (the index finger symbolizes the ego, so it is not to touch the beads). Once I got to the tasseled *meru* bead, I would go back and repeat the mantra another 108 times. Each day I did 10 *malas,* so after about three and a half months, I had completed the *purush charana* and was soon after initiated by Swamiji, who gave me a personal mantra.

The effect this practice had on me is difficult to assess but the message of the mantra (which, while I was repeating the Sanskrit form of the Gayatri Mantra, I was simultaneously remembering Swamiji's English translation) has become an integral dimension of my way of being. I repeated it aloud to my children when they were very young – to soothe them when they were upset and as they were going to sleep. And I repeat it to this day as I do my daily breath practice (*nadi shodhanam* – alternate nostril breathing) as a way of regulating the out and in breaths.

Along with the way the depth of Raja Yoga was instilled in us, the non-dualistic system of Advaita Vedanta was, like osmosis, infused into our minds. The many classes and workshops we attended, the reading material available for us to study -- from ancient Vedic texts to more recent commentaries and lectures as well as countless discussions we had among ourselves – originated in the perspective that there really is only one mind and we are all essentially connected, in some way like what the internet provides.

As Swamiji was preparing to leave for India one late autumn day, he invited "the boys" to his office. He proceeded to discuss the chores and projects which each of us was expected to work on, but when he came to me, he said, "You will come and go as you please." What a surprise! And that is what I did. I went out into the world feeling as if I'd gone through a kind of basic training that prepared me for the rest of my life.

When I consider now, how that time at the yoga institute affected me, the context of basic training as it is usually understood within the framework of military service, offers an interesting contrast when reflecting upon metaphors drawn from *A Course in Miracles* – the battleground and the classroom. Within this study, there are two thought systems in our mind. First, when we perceive the world from the ego thought system, the world appears as a battleground. Here we are vulnerable to attacks from our perceived enemies. We defend against attack by and through counterattack and the cycle of violence is perpetuated repeatedly. On the other hand, when we perceive the world from the thought system of the Holy Spirit, we recognize that everything that occurs in our interactions is about love. We either express love or we call for love. Identifying with our nature as Spirit, we know we're invulnerable and don't take anything personally. Our response is the same in either case – we respond with love whether the other is expressing love or calling for love. In this latter thought system, life then becomes a classroom for learning that everything which occurs in our interactions is about love.[28] Having been newly guided by Swamiji to the understanding that our true nature is spiritual and eternal, I was ready to step into the classroom.

After again hitchhiking to California, the East Coast and then back to the Midwest, I found myself returning to the yoga institute where I met Rise, my wife, and together we were invited to the new headquarters of the yoga institute in another state. Having holistically strengthened my foundation and clarified my sense of purpose during my "boot camp/basic training" as an ashramite in the first yoga institute, I was ready to resume the *ashrama* of student (*Brahmacharya*). Having also become a husband, I was beginning the householder/career (*Grihastha*) ashrama. There are four stages (*ashrama)* of spiritual growth in the yoga system, with the third being retired (*Vanaprastha*) and lastly, becoming a renunciant of worldly things (*Sannyasa*). Although Rise and I lived on the institute campus and were engaged in the community there, it was clearly no longer an ashram experience.

We were committed to the lifestyle grounded in yoga and meditation. We enjoyed the experience of growing together as like-minded seekers sharing a common purpose. For us as a couple, the focus for Rise and I was to establish careers and a family. Rise found work in the city where I enrolled at the university and completed my Bachelor of Science degree in Human Services. Not only were the required theology and philosophy courses taught by Jesuits quite fascinating, but the focus upon developing counseling skills and other practical aspects of the helping profession in my major coursework proved very helpful in later years. Once we knew our first child was on the way, Risë and I moved into an apartment in a small town and upon graduation, I began working for the public welfare department. As with all my other work experiences, my public welfare job provided an education rich in depth and scope interpersonally, professionally and spiritually. It was during this time that I also continued my formal education, attending a graduate program in Eastern Studies and Comparative Psychology, in affiliation with the university. My internship and practicum for this program was done at a hospital. This gave me an opportunity to integrate the many concepts and skills I had learned at the undergraduate level. I applied these concepts and skills to co-leading group therapy for patients as well as individual therapy with a few other patients.

Even before resigning from the hospital job, I began attending workshops on hypnotherapy, including some conducted by colleagues of Milton Erickson. Erickson was a unique psychiatrist who brought hypnotherapy to the high level of credibility and respect it carries today among medical professionals. A few years later, I was trained by the Upledger Institute in Cranial Sacral Therapy and Somato emotional release – modalities which, along with hypnotherapy, greatly enhanced the quality of my work as a psychotherapist. While still at the hospital, however, I had begun studying *A Course in Miracles*. In the context of delving deeply into the minds and hearts of my patients, utilizing their extensive psycho-social and legal records as background material for my work with them, I was coincidentally framing their journey in the perspective of true forgiveness which the Course reveals.

As an aide, I chose to spend countless hours joining them in their daily routine – walking in the recreation yard, playing pool and accompanying them as they visited family or friends who were able to make the long trip to see their loved ones. Rather than simply sitting and maintaining "security" as defined by my job requirements, I chose to engage with them as fellow human/spiritual beings. The depth of my interactions with them went beyond the superficial role of guarding them from a safe distance to cultivating a qualitative depth in speaking and listening to them such that real trust was engendered between us. This trust gave rise to their sharing innermost thoughts and feelings with me which were hitherto not revealed to anyone else.

An underlying theme that has repeatedly surfaced in my reflection upon this work is that while my intention as a psychotherapist has been to enrich the lives of my clients by teaching them various ways to reduce stress, thereby inspiring joy and freedom in their lives, the quality of my *own* life undergoes a corresponding enhancement. I have often voiced my sense that the reciprocal gain of transformation arising between my clients and myself, makes the exchange of money for my services – while a practical necessity – more of an amusing irony. I must emphasize how, for me, engaging in my work as a psychotherapist, has been as much a process of facilitating the process of growth for others as it has been about my own. So, whenever I find a therapeutic modality or another systemic approach to self-transformation, I embrace it with this dual dynamic in mind.

One treasure trove of such self-transformative information for me has been the tapes and CDs offered by Sounds True located in Boulder, Colorado. Beginning in the late '80s, I ordered and devoured the works of Caroline Myss, Pema Chodron, Jack Kornfield and many other luminaries. Repetitive listening of these audio materials has brought at least some of their insights into the fabric of my being. Other seminal works which have been a source of raising consciousness, as well as becoming pillars of the Namaste Principle, follow. Stephen Covey's *The Seven Habits of Highly Effective People,* along with several related books by Covey, present a holistic guide which draws upon the practical wisdom of great thinkers over the past 300 years. Covey has distilled the essence of what habits of these historic leaders led them to achieve success. Furthermore, he presents this essence in a format which allows readers extraordinary access to utilize these habits in their own lives.

Psychologist Marshall Rosenberg devoted his life to resolving the dichotomy between the propensity toward resurgent conflict within human beings leading to aggression and violence and the opposite tendency within the human heart toward acceptance and compassion. His *Non-Violent Communication: A Language of Life* offers practical guidelines which, for those drawn toward this path, will significantly reduce the level of antagonism and animosity often arising in their interpersonal interactions. At the very least, such effort along Rosenberg's guidelines, may even bring about what Covey calls "win-win resolutions"[29]– a synergistic outcome that leaves both previously defensive, combative sides happy in the awareness of being truly seen and heard for who they are.

I had integrated Non-Violent Communication (NVC) into my counseling practice with good results when I was invited to co-lead an anger management program which had been conducted at the mental health agency where I was working. As I observed the way the other therapist was conducting the group process, I realized how ideally Rosenberg's NVC would enhance the program's success. I also introduced basic yogic breathing and relaxation techniques to help the group gain greater mindfulness in practicing the four steps of NVC. These steps are:[30]

1) When faced with an emotionally charged situation, ask yourself, "What's alive in me?" – that is, what are my feelings? what is the unmet need triggering these feelings? And what would I prefer the other person do?

2) With an "I – statement" express the feeling(s) – for example, "I feel angry, sad, scared, frustrated, "etc. without blaming the other.

3) Identify the unmet need such as "My need to be treated with respect is not being met."

4) Make a request without threatening or demanding such as "Would you please lower your voice and listen to my side of the story?

At first, many of the group members often say, "Nobody I know talks like that!" or they express some other form of resistance. However, once they get a sense of how they can use their own words and learn how to retreat from the attack/defense mode, most people begin to adjust their communication style to be less antagonistic. Again, the more they practice the relaxation and breath exercises, the more skillful they become at NVC.

Back in 2000, Byron Katie first published her book, *Loving What Is*, in which she shares the psycho-spiritual system to which she awakened and dubbed "The Work."[31] I picked it up, studied it and soon began applying its principles in both my personal and professional life. "The Work", as Katie presents it, guides us into potentially life-altering self-inquiry. As we find ourselves in a stressful situation, we pause to look at whom or what we are judging critically. Then, we do "the work": observe how you judge your neighbor (identifying as many levels of "should," "shouldn't," "supposed to," "not supposed to," etc.) and then ask four questions:

1) Is it true?
2) Can I know it's absolutely true?
3) How do I react when I think that thought?
4) Who would I be without that thought?

After exploring these four questions, we do the "turnaround" in which we proactively address our own responsibility in a provocative situation.[32] I compare the turnaround to looking at the finger-pointing gesture we so often make and then, we notice there's only one finger pointing at the accused, yet three fingers pointing back at us! As the name of Katie's system implies, this IS *work – the work of awakening,* and yet, as I often say, "Waking up is hard to do!" The key, as always, is our willingness to engage in the process of self-examination and stay with it to transform life as we have known it.

One of the people who had promoted Katie's book was Eckhart Tolle, the author of *The Power of Now* – the book which catapulted him into the public eye. I found him to be remarkably sophisticated in his understanding of the spiritual life. In an excerpt from his book, *A New Earth*, we see some of his fundamental principles:

"Be absolutely present in what you do and sense the alert, alive stillness within you in the background of the activity. You will soon find that what you do in such a state of heightened awareness, instead of being stressful, tedious, or irritating, is actually becoming enjoyable. To be more precise, what you are enjoying is not really the outward action but the inner dimension of consciousness that flows into the action. This is finding the joy of Being in what you are doing...The new earth arises as more and more people discover that their main purpose in life is to bring the light of consciousness into this world and so use whatever they do as a vehicle for consciousness. The joy of Being is the joy of being conscious. Awakened consciousness then takes over from ego and begins to run your life. You may then find that an activity that you have been engaged in for a long time naturally begins to expand into something much bigger when it becomes empowered by consciousness...But don't let it go to your head, because up there is where a remnant of ego may be hiding. You are still an ordinary human. What is extraordinary is what comes through you into this world. But that essence you share with all beings."[33]

Six of these systems – Raja Yoga, *A Course in Miracles, Non-Violent Communication, The Four Agreements, The 7 Habits of Highly Effective People and The Work* -- I've integrated into *Living the Namaste Principle.* They share essential elements: carefully, mindfully looking at the truth of existence; drawing upon a deep respect of self and others in interpersonal relationships (i.e. applying the Golden Rule); relying upon discernment rather than condemnation in observing human affairs – all grounded in a view of humanity's inherent goodness or divinity. Rather than taking the view of human nature as sinful and needing punishment, we may see human error as mistakes in need of correction. The messages of Katie and Tolle especially exemplify this deeply spiritual congruency.

Don Miguel Ruiz, who is known for his exposition of *The Four Agreements*, draws from the wisdom of the ancient, shamanic Toltec tradition, a lineage of teachings extending back to Mayan and Incan cultures. The Four Agreements are:[34]

1) *Be impeccable in giving your word.*
2) *Don't make assumptions.*
3) *Don't take anything personally.*
4) *In everything you do, do your best.*

His guidance in applying the principles inherent in *The Four Agreements* rings true when seen in the light of the most sophisticated, psychological/spiritual systems. As with so many other systems, there's a deceptive simplicity in *The Four Agreements.* Yet, when we attempt to live according to these agreements, we realize how challenging it is to do so. However, as with *The Work, Non-Violent Communication, The Seven Habits* and *A Course in Miracles*, we understand that to the degree we follow the essential principles of *The Four Agreements*, our lives will become less stressful and happier.

While considering the congruency of psycho-spiritual traditions and concepts, it is somewhat comforting to know that, no matter from which corner of the planet a particular system has arisen, when we filter out specific cultural, psychological, and socio-economic artifacts, we find the same essential truth. The message is about love and inclusiveness – the acknowledgement that, no matter where we are born or what our status in life, underneath the guise of these diverse artifacts of being human, we are all the same, we are interconnected - one in the Spirit, in truth, One Spirit manifesting in many forms.

By attuning our lives to such systems as reviewed here (and I think these merely represent only a few examples of the countless systems that have arisen and are yet to arise), we may awaken to a way of being grounded in love, harmony, beauty and truth. These qualities of life are what distinguish the Namaste Principle. Maybe you call it by another name? The names and forms are diverse, the essence is the same. Identified with the names and forms, we find reason to argue, divide, fight and start wars. Identified with the ground of essence, we let go of fear and judgment and embrace compassion, mercy and love.

Glossary

A Course in Miracles – A psychologically-oriented system of spirituality which consists of three books: a text presenting the metaphysics of the Course; a Workbook for Students; and a Manual for Teachers.

Advaita Vedanta – Considered to be the most sophisticated of the seven systems of Indian philosophy, it is non-dualistic in approach and comprises the essence of the ancient Vedic scriptures.

Ahimsa – A Sanskrit word for non-violence or non-injuriousness; this is the first of five *yamas* (restraints) that form the first limb of Raja Yoga, also known as *Ashtanga* (*asht* = 8 and *anga* = limb) Yoga. Many people consider *ahimsa* to be the foundation of the practice of yoga in general.

Alcoholics Anonymous – A system devised by two friends known as Bill W. and Dr. Bob who, as alcoholics yearned for a way to cure a disease that historically, rarely responded to treatment. The psychoanalyst, Carl G. Jung, informed Dr. Bob that his illness, although of a physical nature, could only be cured through a spiritual process. Thus began Alcoholics Anonymous, where those suffering from this disease joined together anonymously to follow the Twelve Step Program: grounded in the acceptance that, as a limited ego, one is powerless over addiction, one then begins to surrender to a "higher power" while engaging in a "fearless moral inventory" to make amends where necessary for any wrongdoing committed while under the influence of alcohol. As one reaches the eleventh step of the program, there comes a spiritual awakening followed by a determination to assist others in the recovery process.

Aldous Huxley – (B. July 26, 1894 – D. November 22, 1963) A British novelist and philosopher whose works include *Brave New World, Island* and *Doors of Perception.* His writings and philosophy were influenced by his association with The Vedanta Society of Southern California.

Aparigraha – This is the fifth of the *yamas* (restraints) in the Raja Yoga system which in Sanskrit is translated as non-possessiveness or detachment, that is non-identification with one's possessions. It has been said that a beggar may be more attached to his bowl and sandals than a wealthy person to his belongings.

Ashram – In Indian culture, a place of spiritual retreat like the Western concept of a monastery.

Ashrama – One of four stages of life presented in the Dharma Sutra which follows a progression of experiences and learning during each stage, culminating in spiritual awakening. These stages are: Brahmacharya (age: birth to 24 years) where one focuses upon studying all that will prepare him/her for the next stage of life: Grihastha (age: 24-48 years old) where one is known as a householder during the time when career and family are the primary objectives. Vanaprashtha (age: 48-72 years old) is the stage of retirement when a person hands down household responsibility to the next generation while gradually withdrawing from the world. The final *ashrama* is Sannyasa (age: 73-death) when one renounces all material and worldly interests and focuses solely on spiritual attainment.

Asteya – This is the third *yama* (restraint) of the Raja Yoga system which means non-stealing even to the point of not taking credit for something one has not done.

Beingness – That state or quality of being grounded in our true, spiritual nature – eternal, invulnerable – where one relates to everyone and everything in the world as a unified whole, not separate parts.

Bhagavad Gita – Translated from Sanskrit as "Song of God" this is a classic, Hindu spiritual text which is part of a larger epic called the Mahabharata, and which relates a story of a war between the Pandavas and the Kauravas, family and friends alike. Through a dialogue between the two main characters in the story – Lord Krishna and Arjuna – a teaching is presented as an example of how to apply the principles of various forms of yoga to the responsibilities and duties of life and its challenges.

Buddha – A person who has awakened from life's illusory nature to become enlightened and free from human suffering. Siddhartha Gautama is considered the first one to have attained this state and is acknowledged as the original source of Buddhist teachings.

Cranial Sacral Therapy (CST) – A treatment discovered by osteopath, Dr. William Sutherland and later developed by osteopath, Dr. John Upledger. Gently manipulating the rhythmic flow of cerebrospinal fluid throughout the body, CST helps detect and adjust imbalances in the nervous system.

Four Noble Truths – Understanding set forth by Siddhartha Gautama in order to attain the state of being a Buddha: the world is a place of suffering; there is a cause of suffering; there is a way to gain freedom from suffering; lastly, the way to cease suffering is the eight-fold path of right view, right intention, right speech, right action, right livelihood, right effort, right mindfulness and right concentration.

Gayatri Mantra – This is a highly revered mantra from the Rig Veda, an ancient Indian collection of sacred Sanskrit hymns dating back to the second millennium B.C.

Hatha Yoga – A form of yoga which focuses on supporting spiritual unfoldment through disciplining the body through postures or exercises and breath practices. "Ha" means "sun" and "Tha" means "moon" so this form of yoga is considered as a means of balancing the different energies within our being.

Ishvara Pranidhana – The fifth of the *niyamas* (observances) in the Raja Yoga system which expresses surrendering to the presence of the Divine. In common parlance, "Let go, Let God," it is comparable in that one can transcend the individual ego by opening to the unlimited realm of Spirit.

Karma – Translated from Sanskrit, this means action and is understood in the yoga system as a principle of cause and effect – one's actions have an effect or consequence. In Hindu culture, *karma* is associated with the process of attending to our positive and negative actions from our current life as well as from past lives to transcend the limiting nature of our actions.

Mala – In Sanskrit it means a "garland" of beads used to train one's mind by repetition (*japa*) of a sacred word or sound many times with great concentration.

Mantra – A sacred utterance – a word or group of words – repeated during prayer or meditation, to support one's spiritual growth. Often, when one takes initiation -- that is, commits to being taught by a spiritual master -- one receives a special mantra from that spiritual teacher.

Meru bead – A tasseled bead on the *mala* which marks the beginning and end of a cycle of repetitions of mantra; *meru* means "mountain" or "*guru*".

Nadi Shodhanam – One of the breath practices in the Raja Yoga system known as alternate nostril breathing whereby the breath is exhaled and inhaled alternately through each nostril with the other nostril closed to balance and harmonize the flow of energy between the two hemispheres of the brain, creating a calming, clearing effect on one's being. *Nadi* is a subtle energy channel like neural pathways throughout the human body and *shodhan* means cleansing.

Niyamas – Besides the *yamas* (restraints) in the Raja Yoga system, these are observances which serve to establish the foundation for other dimensions of Raja Yoga practice: cleanliness or purity (*saucha*), contentment (*santosha*), austerity (*tapas*), self-study (*svadhyaya*), and surrender (*ishwara pranidhana*).

Patanjali – Codified the theory and practice of Raja Yoga in the text called the Yoga Sutras, a compilation of 196 verses describing the steps in the Raja Yoga system, along with a discussion of the various states of consciousness one might experience as one practices this system.

Ram Dass – Formerly known as Richard Alpert, Ph.D., is an American spiritual teacher and author, who following his research at Harvard University with Timothy Leary, travelled to India where he found his guru, Neem Karoli Baba.

Ramana Maharshi – (B. 1879 – D. 1950) A Hindu sage who was known for his experience of enlightenment through a process of self-inquiry which formed the basis of his teachings.

Sanskrit – An ancient Indic language in which the Hindu scriptures and classical Indian epic poems are written and from which many northern Indian languages are derived.

Shanti – A Sanskrit word which means peace and conveys a state of being mentally and spiritually at peace, with enough knowledge and understanding to keep oneself strong in the face of discord or stress.

So Hum – A Hindu mantra which means "I am That" in which one is reminded of one's divine nature.

Somato Emotional Release (SER) – A therapy distinguished by Dr. John Upledger involving gentle pressure upon different areas of the body within which energy may have been blocked or imbalanced due to trauma. The process may lead to a release and rebalancing of energy within oneself.

Sutra – Sanskrit for a string or thread yet is usually applied to an aphorism or other teaching which is part of the ancient religious traditions of South Asia.

Swami(ji) – In Sanskrit this translates as a person who has mastered the smaller self and one's habit patterns so that the eternal Self rules the individual rather than the ego. "Ji" is a term of reverence or respect attached to the end of the master's name or title.

Tao Te Ching – A classical Chinese text credited to the sixth century sage, Lao Tzu which is the fundamental text for both philosophical and religious Taoism.

Tasbih – A string of beads used for repetitive prayer or mantra in middle Eastern spirituality and cultures like the *mala* of Hindus or the Catholic rosary.

Upanishads – Ancient Sanskrit text which are part of the Vedas and contains some of the central philosophical concepts and ideas of Hinduism, some of which are shared with Buddhism and Jainism.

Viveka – Sanskrit term which means right understanding or discriminative knowledge differentiates between the real and the unreal, truth and illusion, eternal and temporary, and Self and non-Self realities.

Zen Buddhism – A school of Mahayana Buddhism that emerged in China bout 15 centuries ago where it was called Ch'an Buddhism. Derived from the Sanskrit term *Dhyana* – meditation – Ch'an, in its Japanese iteration, is the same as Zen – both expressing the essential nature of Buddhism: to cultivate a mind absorbed in meditation upon the real, the unchanging, the eternal.

Endnotes

1   Foundation for Inner Peace, *A Course in Miracles: The Advent of a Great Awakening* (Mill Valley, CA.: Foundation for A Course in Miracles, 2007), Text, 20.

2   Bo Lozoff, *We're All Doing Time: A Guide to Getting Free* (Durham, NC.: Human Kindness Foundation, 1985).

3   Daniel Ladinsky, *I Heard God Laughing – Renderings of Hafiz* (Walnut Creek, CA.: Sufism Reoriented, 1996), 111.

4   Note: This translation of the Gayatri Mantra was presented to the students at the yoga institute by Swami Rama as his own. There are other versions, yet I have found this one to be quite pure and transformative.

5   I came to appreciate the richness of the word "enthusiasm" (and how perfectly it expressed what I felt in that moment) when I heard Wayne Dyer years later define it as "being in God." Webster's Unabridged Dictionary refers to the Greek "enthousiasmos" translated as "possession by a god" with a variation of "entheos", i.e. "having a god within."

6   Robert Heinlein, *Stranger in a Strange Land* (New York: Penguin Random House, 1991), 265-266.

7   Kahlil Gibran, *The Prophet* (New York: Knopf, 1970), 17.

8   Stephen R. Covey, *The 7 Habits of Highly Effective People* (New York: Fireside, 1990), 95.

9   Id., 235.

10 Id., 261.

11 Harville Hendrix, Ph.D., *Getting the Love You Want* (New York: Harper Perennial, 1990), 256.

12 Marshall B. Rosenberg, Ph.D., *Non-Violent Communication: A Language of Life* (Encinitas, CA.: Puddle Dancers Press, 2015).

13 Ross W. Greene, *The Explosive Child* (New York: Harper Collins, 1998).

14 Richard Alpert, Ph.D., *Remember: Be Here Now* (New Mexico: Lama Foundation, 1971).

15 William G. Wilson and Dr. Bob Smith, *Alcoholics Anonymous, Third Edition* (New York: Alcoholics Anonymous World Services, Inc., 1976), p.64.

16 Plato, "Plato's Apology of Socrates," www.sjsu.edu/people/james.lindahl/courses/Phil70A/s3/apology.pdf, 20, 38a.

17 *Alcoholics Anonymous, Third Edition*, p.85.

18 John Bullaro, Ph.D., "A New Beginning," The SloCoast Journal, Issue 43, (January 2013): http://slocoastjournal.net/docs/archives/2013/jan/pages/human_condition.html.

19 John Muir, *My First Summer in the Sierra*, (San Francisco: Sierra Club Books, 1988), p.110.

20 Thomas Kuhn, *The Structure of Scientific Revolutions* (Chicago: University of Chicago Press, 1962).

21 Malcolm Gladwell, *The Tipping Point* (New York, Boston, London: Little, Brown and Company, 2000), 5.

22 Foundation for Inner Peace, *A Course in Miracles Text* (Mill Valley, CA.: Foundation for A Course in Miracles, 2007), 402-403.

23 Pierre Teilhard de Chardin, *The Phenomenon of Man* (Toronto, Canada: The Great Library Collections by R.P. Pryne, 2015).

24 Phillipians 4:7 (English Standard Version).

25 Viktor E. Frankl, *Man's Search for Meaning* (New York: Simon and Schuster, 1963) 106.

26 Ken Keyes, Jr., *Handbook to Higher Consciousness, 3rd Edition* (Berkeley, CA: Living Love Center, 1973), 87.

27 I.K.Taimni, *The Science of Yoga, 4th Edition* (Wheaton, IL: Theosophical Publishing House, A Quest Book, 1975), 206-230.

28 Kenneth Wapnick, Ph.D., *Forgiveness and Jesus: The Meeting Place of A Course in Miracles and Christianity* (Mill Valley, CA: Foundation for A Course in Miracles, 1983), 66.

29 Stephen R. Covey, *The 7 Habits of Highly Effective People, 1st Edition* (New York: Fireside, 1989), 204.

30 Marshall B. Rosenberg, Ph.D., *Non-Violent Communication: A Language of Life, 3rd Edition* (Encinitas, CA: Puddle Dancers Press, 2015), 6.

31 Byron Katie and Stephen Mitchell, *Loving What Is: Four Questions That Can Change Your Life* (New York: Harmony Books, 2002), 15.

32 Ibid., 15.

33 Eckhart Tolle, *A New Earth* (London, UK: Penguin Group, 2008), 299-300.

34 Don Miguel Ruiz, *The Four Agreements: A Practical Guide to Personal Freedom* (San Rafael, CA: Amber-Allen Publishing, 1997), 25, 47, 63 and 75.